Alec Go...

MORGAN'S MEMORIES

C000274917

Good luck
John Morgan

Morgan's Memories

John Morgan

Illustrated by Matt Latchford

Smith
Settle

First published in 2001 by
Smith Settle Ltd
Ilkley Road
Otley
West Yorkshire
LS21 3JP

© John Morgan 2001
Illustrations © Matt Latchford 2001

All rights reserved. No part of this book may be
reproduced, stored or introduced into a retrieval system,
or transmitted in any form or by any means (electronic,
mechanical, photocopying, recording or otherwise)
without the permission of Smith Settle Ltd.

The right of John Morgan to be identified as author of
this work has been asserted by him in accordance
with the Copyright, Designs and Patents Act 1988.

ISBN 1 85825 157 5

Set in Monotype Sabon

Designed, printed and bound by
SMITH SETTLE
Ilkley Road, Otley, West Yorkshire LS21 3JP

Contents

When Les Hit the Right Note	1
Dropping a Clanger	3
The Birds and the Bees	6
Any Road Up	10
Moggy with a Nose for News	13
Dressing for the Occasion	15
Fire, Brimstone and Good Old Mr Lazarus	18
Old Snecklifters and New Beggars	21
Having a Go with Wilfred	23
The Busy Bees Next Door	26
Open All Hours	29
Tales of the Dark Ages	31
The Last Resort	33
Sweet and Spicy Memories	35
Hair Today and None Tomorrow	37
Tanks for the Memory	40
Such Devoted Sisters	43
A Spring in my Step	46
Fiery Fred's Gentle Delivery	48
Mavis Had a Word for It	51
Veritable Feast on a Platter	54
Where There's a Will	56
Brushing Shoulders with Royalty	59
The Hard Men of Soccer	62
Getting Around to It	65
The Job of a Lifetime	68
King of the Tipsters	71
A Brush with Destiny	74
Nappy Days	77
Oh, my Aching Pride	79
The Silent Heroes of Soapland	82
On the Fiddle	84
Watch Your Language	86

A Miracle Cure for Heartache   88
The 'Lucky, Lucky, Lucky' Grandad   91
Choked ... by my Underwear   94
Panacea for a Few Pence   97
The Bug Hutch   100
Memoirs of a Brylcreem Boy   102
When Opportunity Knocked   105
The Worm Turns   107
Pulling the Other One   110
Town of Good Manners   111
Having a Beano   112
An Elusive Crock of Gold   114
The Virtues of Home   117

Foreword

Those were the days, weren't they? Back in the early nineteen-fifties? When four up-and-coming journalists honed their skills — Whitelocks; the Whip; the Ostlers; Polly's Bar and any other Leeds city-centre watering-hole that took their fancy. Peter O'Toole, trainee photographer at the *Yorkshire Post*, Keith Waterhouse, on the reporting staff at the *Yorkshire Evening Post*, Willis Hall, beavering away on the *Sporting Pink* — and then there was John Morgan, another *Yorkshire Evening Post* man.

The first three of those south Leeds lads left the city not long after to try their hands in London. The fourth, John Morgan (Castleford born, but raised on Leeds's Gipton estate) stayed behind to write about horse-racing, boxing, and, indeed, all and everything under the Yorkshire sun that took his fancy — and a good job too, for otherwise this hugely entertaining book would never have seen the light of day.

Coming back to the North, a score of years or so ago, one of the first acquaintanceships that I renewed was that of my old journalistic sparring partner. Nothing gives me greater pleasure, in these my bus-pass days, than to meet up with John, be it over a day's cricket at the Yorkshire County Cricket Club; an afternoon at the South Leeds Stadium (for we are both committed Hunslet Hawks men); or a longish lunch at a favourite restaurant.

Wherever the venue, as old friends are wont to do, we contemplate past times and mull over all manner of things such as: kali; Woolton pie; Sirdani; Locust Beans; the *'Tisher*; *Chick's Own*; fever grates and trunnel pies ...

If all or any of these subjects tug at your memory strings, then this book is right up your ginnel. If not, then don't despair — read on: by the time you reach the final page, you may not be a great deal wiser about any or all of those intriguing items but, and much more important, you will have smiled and chuckled and laughed a lot along the way.

Willis Hall

Preface

'We were poor — even our butler was poor!' guffawed the after-dinner speaker with little response from the audience. But he touched a raw nerve if not the funny bone for many who recall with mixed feelings the good-old-bad-old-days. There was a hand-to-mouth existence for many impoverished families but laughter and a keen sense of humour compensated for a paucity of material riches. The gift to giggle has so often been a safety valve in times of adversity, and that is why this fortunate author can reflect on the past with smiling affection and no lack of nostalgia.

'We were poor — even our butler was poor.' We didn't have much but what we had we shared. You are welcome to a generous portion of Morgan's Memories.

My wife The Lovely Maureen has a terrible memory. She never forgets a thing whereas I have a photographic memory but occasionally forget to take off the lens cap.

The 14th June 2002 is a date it would be wrong of me to overlook. It marks the fiftieth anniversary of my marriage to Maureen and, with that golden occasion in mind, I dedicate this book to her.

Dedicated to my wife Maureen

When Les Hit the Right Note

It was at a wedding in Armley, Leeds, where a mental picture of Les Dawson's rubbery face and musical antics came to mind. He had nothing to do with the nuptial ceremony. But the organ player unwittingly produced a life-like impersonation of Les tinkling the keys at his excruciating best. Do you remember how Les deliberately hit false notes, played out of tune, and made his audience wince, and roar with laughter?

The organist produced a similar performance, but not on purpose. He was simply bad. We tried to sing to the discordant accompaniment but it was impossible. After several false starts we surrendered and endured the blood-curdling thumping of wrong notes with muted mirth. It could have ruined the wedding. We were all embarrassed. But within minutes of leaving the church we saw the hilarious side.

It was at the old Dragonara Hotel, Leeds, where I told Les the story. It opened the floodgates for a string of piano, organ and wedding tales from the droll comic. Les later lifted the lid of Bert Gaunt's pianoforte and provided an impromptu concert for a group of receptive and, I confess, slightly inebriated journalists.

I have only recently taken the advice of the rather sad-faced clown whose premature passing robbed us of an inimitable talent. Who else but laconic Les could have written:

'Many ills have beset mankind — plague, famine and pestilence. The abyss of inflation yawns and yet dear John there is a greater folly of man's own making. I refer of course to the Garden Party ...

This summer I have tottered through at least a score of these frightening confrontations ... the dreadful thing about these "do's" is that they are all the same. They follow a pattern of lunacy so beloved of our island race.

A Southport vicar with flared nostrils and a bald head came to see me. As he walked into my dressing room he looked like a theological Kojak. He shook my hand with a paw that was not unlike a mechanical grab and before I could plead advanced migraine he booked me to open his fête.

For two days I wrote down a series of gags. Sleep eluded me. The thought of the fête tortured my imagination. I tossed and turned, much to the annoyance of the wife who works late at the St Anne's Karate School. The wages are rotten but she gets plenty of backhanders.

The day dawned. I was greeted by a fierce grey spinster who poked me playfully in the ribcage and sent me reeling into a deceased laburnum shrub. I trotted at her heels and entered the hall where hot children with wide eyes and toffee-stained teeth closed in on me like a pack of savage dingoes.

I was introduced by a florid lady with ill-fitting dentures. They dropped down like a plastic portcullis. I declared the fête open and fled ...

As I reached the safety of my car I heard the vicar holler: "We should have booked Arthur Askey ..."'

Les has gone but he will not be forgotten. I will remember him at the next church fête and whenever the organ plays.

Dropping a Clanger

There are certain things a chap simply does not do. For instance, one does not arrive at a formal reception in open-neck shirt, sweater, anorak and crêpe-soled creepers, does one? But I did.

Blackpool beckoned and I was invited to a function with the comforting advice: 'Don't go to any trouble. We don't stand on ceremony. Everyone is friendly and it will be nice to see you.'

I entered the ornate Winter Gardens ballroom and — to my eternal horror — every male sported a dinner jacket, bow-tie and patent leather shoes. And every lady twirled in a frilly frock to gaze at the unwitting gatecrasher. Have you ever had one of those crimson blushes that start at your collar-stud and skidaddle to the roots of your widow's peak? I had that and more. I wanted to flee. But welcoming handshakes halted the retreat, and I settled in a darkened corner and gazed at a sea of dancers as a wave of nostalgia washed away my initial embarrassment.

I spent many teenage hours dancing to music played on the Mighty Wurlitzer by Reginald Dixon at the Blackpool Tower ballroom. But there was always extra magic at the Winter Gardens where Ted Heath and his band stole the limelight.

Pimple-faced youths stood in groups. They dared each other to approach dainty wallflowers. And we shyly declined as the girls — seated on red plush chairs — waited in vain for the reticent male of the species to make his elegant advance. More dashing lads, fortified with halves of shandy, eventually plucked up courage to request: 'May I have this dance please?' If they had seen a couple of American films, they usually drawled: 'Do you wanna shake a leg, babe? Do you feel groovy, kid? Okay snake, let's glide!'

I was more the reluctant type. But even if you didn't recognise a tango from a quickstep, you were transported to another planet with the music of the era. Ted Heath fronted musicians including George Chisholm on trombone, Jack Parnell on drums, and handsome Canadian Paul Carpenter providing the vocals. A couple of annual holidays later we still danced to Ted's big band, but the singing came from Lita

Rosa, Denis Lotis and, of course, the late Dickie Valentine, who was responsible for more wails of adoration from lovesick girls than any other crooner of that period.

I was lost in the reverie. And it was near midnight when I made my escape from the Winter Gardens. I strolled along the front properly dressed, and at peace with the world. And then I spotted it — a name in lights — and another signal for a bout of memories.

Flickering bulbs told us that the sensational superstar P J Proby was appearing tonight and every night. And my thoughts flashed to the years when clubland was at its zenith and the capital of the entertainment world was Greaseborough Working Men's Club, near Doncaster. It was there I met P J Proby.

Concert secretaries were omnipotent, and the chap at Greaseborough was powerful and compère to boot. He attained the exalted position because of a connection with showbusiness. During the war he was wounded and taken to an army hospital. It was there that he shook hands with Vera Lynn, and this made him the ideal fellow to run the show at Greaseborough.

On the night P J Proby was billed to appear, there was an undercurrent of ill-feeling. It was obvious that the 'con sec' was not happy. But in time-honoured tradition the show had to go on. And he strode to the microphone to introduce the first act. We expected Karl Denver and his trio. But our man with the mike blew, tapped on the apparatus and hollered 'testing, testing'. He then ignored the howling feedback to inform us that the stage would be taken by 'Karl Denby and his tryo'. The Deep River Boys — a popular American group of velvet-throated singers — followed Karl and they smiled with cheerful acceptance at their introduction, which does not bear repeating in these more enlightened, politically correct days.

We then waited for the top of the bill. You could bite the atmosphere. Ructions were threatened and we were not disappointed. The 'con sec' grabbed the mike, tossed the trailing lead over his shoulder, and with a shout of 'All round the room' he silenced the expectant customers.

'Now you all know I've been away on holiday for two weeks at Blackpool with my missus', he yelled. 'And the next

turn was booked OVVER MY 'EAD! I don't like him and YOU won't like him. And if he splits his pants like he did at Wakefield last week, I'm paying him up. Come on and do your best Pee Jay Probate!'

We howled with glee. And we hollered as the gyrating rock-and-roller pranced about the stage, singing, strumming, and threatening to burst out of his skin-tight trousers. I will never forget the sight or the night.

The Birds and the Bees

Helen is an angelic seven year old with an inquisitive nature. She is at the stage when children — we are assured — have reached the age of reason. She demands answers to her searching questions.

Helen occupied her regular place at the family dining table last Sunday and, just as the billowing Yorkshire puddings were being served, she produced a conversation stopper.

'Mum, will you tell me please where I come from.'

There followed what one can only and — probably appropriately — describe as 'a pregnant pause'.

Mum turned pink as the pork she had left for browning. Dad spluttered into his handkerchief. And a couple of stifled titters from Helen's more mature brother and sister added to the general confusion. Mum and dad exchanged embarrassed glances. This was not the time for a talk on reproduction. This was not the occasion or location for a discussion on the instruction from the Good Lord to 'go out and multiply'. This was not an ideal moment for a discourse on the birds and bees.

Red-faced dad coughed to clear his throat. He murmured: 'Eat your pudding, Helen. We will talk about this later.'

Helen's brother and sister giggled. But Helen is nothing if not an obedient little lassie, and she did as dad instructed.

We had a similar experience when I was a child. It was wartime and my sister Kitty had just reached the age of seven. On her way to school she often practised her reading by looking at the posters on hoardings stretching the length of York Road, Leeds. One notice requested us to 'Dig For Victory' and another advised us that 'Careless Talk Costs Lives'. And she read one which carried a dire warning to the nation's philanderers. It was one she did not understand, but she waited until the family sat down to Sunday lunch before blurting out: 'Dad, what is venereal disease?'

There was an explosion of shocked silence. My mother almost dropped to her knees. She made the sign of the cross on her forehead and chest. She reached for her rosary beads, and our father's first reaction was to shout for soap and water to erase the black mark from his erring infant's tongue. But he cooled and replied simply and rather sadly: 'It is nothing for you to worry about'. I was a more worldly nine year old. But I almost choked on my wartime ration of Sunday meat when Kitty asked that immortal if not immoral poser.

The present generation of juniors — apart from Helen — seems to know all the answers, and I remember the story of brothers Charlie and Jim engaging in a conversation about babies and how the infants came into existence. Jim, the older lad, believed that he knew and he basked in his new-found knowledge. He swanked in front of the younger child and asked: 'Do you know where babies come from, our Charlie?'

'Of course I do, our Jim', he replied. 'They come from under the gooseberry bush because our mam told me.'

'They don't you know', Jim persisted. 'Mam's been having us on. I know for definite where they come from.'

'I've heard that the stork brings them as well', responded Charlie.

'You're wrong again', Jim preened.

'Well, tell me then', Charlie asked in desperation. 'Where do they come from?'

'They come from the chemist's shop', Jim crowed. 'I've just seen the chemist weighing a couple.'

There is another chestnut told about the chap who knocked at a farm door and his summons was answered by a diminutive boy who asked: 'What do you want mister?'

'I want to talk to your dad about your Malcolm and our Lily', the mister hollered.

'I'm sorry he's not here', the boy said. 'He's gone to the market to sell some of our cattle. He won't be back until this evening.'

The mister was obviously not at all pleased. And he thundered: 'Your Malcolm has got my Lily in the family way. She is with child and I want to know what your dad is going to do about it!'

The youngster scratched his head and murmured: 'I can't help you there, mister. I don't know what he will say. But I can tell you that he charges £20 for our bull.'

I must admit that my childhood was pretty sheltered. I didn't know the meaning of some expressions, but I thought I was being fairly adult when I passed on a message to my

mother to tell her that 'Mrs So-and-so has gone into hospital.'
The news was accepted with little or hardly any show of
emotion. But my mother went berserk when I added: 'She's
been confined.' I thought I had been found guilty of the most
heinous of mortal sins. My mother's face registered shock,
horror. Where on earth, she thought, had her innocent cherub
heard that grown-up description of a lady entering the
maternity ward? It was simple really. I was often asked by one
neighbour or another to dash to tell the local midwife Nurse
Payne that a lady 'had started'. It was Nurse Payne who used
the word 'confined'. I suppose it was right coming from her
lips, but not from the mouth of a babe or suckling.

But back to Helen and her query. Did her mum and dad tell
her that babies were fashioned in heaven? Did they explain
that they are God's gift to loving couples who want to share
their grown-up love with a tiny bundle of joy? Did they spin

the yarn about the stork or the gooseberry bush? No they did not.

They realised quite rightly that Helen was growing up. She had attained the age and had so much common sense that it was logical not to beat about the bush — gooseberry or otherwise — but to tell her the truth. Mum and dad did the job properly. They bought the appropriate literature for a child of Helen's age and they went to great pains to answer Helen's question: 'Please tell me where I come from'. Helen listened patiently to her parents and she thanked them quite profusely for their gentle and loving reply to her query. But can you imagine the look on their respective faces when she added:

'I know all that. I know all about babies and how they are made. I wanted to know where I come from because my friend Amanda told me that she comes from Halifax.'

Any Road Up

Putting on airs and graces is a perfectly acceptable pursuit but only if you can carry it through without a verbal gaff. I remember complimenting a lady at Elland Road greyhound stadium on her beautiful dress. She was christened Marlene but preferred the pronounciation 'Marlayna', and she spoke with an exaggerated cut-glass accent.

Marlene sipped a glass of brandy and Babycham — the in-drink at that time — and simpered: 'How sweet of you, darling, to notice. My daddy bought the ensemble in Paris ...' She failed to finish because a chap barged past to plonk a few shillings on his canine fancy. He bumped Marlene in the back and the drink dribbled down her exclusive creation. Marlene reverted to type and hollered: 'Damn them people what does push!'

I thought about Marlene in Betty's in York, where a sweet old lady twittered over her cup of tea and toasted teacake. She was dainty — all lace and face-powder. She maintained a lively conversation, and I mused that she must have had elocution lessons as a child or, as my granny used to say, 'had the penny spent on her'. But the image of finesse and gentility faded. She touched a crumb from the corner of her mouth and resumed her confidential chatter with 'Any road up ... '.

I couldn't believe my ears. But my thoughts went back to a chap who was born in east Leeds, lived at Guiseley, and made his bulky presence felt from one end of the county to the other.

The late Roy Speight was one of Yorkshire's dwindling band of larger-than-life characters. He was entertaining, amusing and could cause mayhem in an empty room. And he often prefixed a story with 'Any road up ...'.

He was a man who kicked against conformity. He made a hobby of pricking pomposity. I remember taking him to Newmarket racecourse where he ate fish and chips out of newspaper in the august members' enclosure. He was eyed with immense suspicion by Brigadier Green, head of security, who followed him to the top storey of the grandstand. Roy hid behind a pillar and when the official arrived he leaped out with a loud 'boo'. The retired military man almost jumped from his bags and bowler.

There was another occasion when pressmen gathered at the Junction, Otley, where the landlord Dick Briggs and his wife Lucy were in the process of leaving to attend a family funeral.

'We have put on a tea for the mourners', Dick said. 'Help yourself to a sandwich or two.'

Roy took full advantage of the invitation. With the help of men from the media he shifted the lot, including a huge cherry cake. And he was swallowing the last morsel when the funeral party returned.

'Any road up', Roy said, 'to cut a long story short — Dick and Lucy were not well pleased.'

I recall Roy quizzing a member of a ballet company in the tap room at the Wellington, which was demolished a few years back. And he asked the startled youth if he had ever appeared in the show about a dying duck. This description of *Swan Lake* did not go down too well with the rather fey dancer.

ANY ROAD UP, IT'LL FINISH SOON.
THIS IS WHERE THE DUCK DIES!

Roy, a fine tenor, was married to Zoe, a key member of the Wallis family, who were resident entertainers at the Peacock, Yeadon, before moving to the Westbourne on the outskirts of Otley. Zoe was a superb pianist, with her sister Pat the lead singer-cum-comedienne, and brother Peter the star of nightly productions which often ran for a couple of hours and more. Peter's quickfire delivery of gags gained him the nickname 'Machine Gun' and he is still cracking one-liners with unbelievable rapidity. Before he opted for a full-time career as a comic, and pub landlord, he worked at Bellows Machine Company, Leeds, helping to manufacture sewing machines. One of Peter's colleagues was a part-time crooner Adrian Hill who won a talent competition at the Shaftesbury Cinema, York Road, Leeds, singing the ballad *With These Hands*. Within a few weeks Adrian became Ronnie Hilton and a heart-throb of the 1950s. Any road up — suffice to say — Peter and Ronnie often took to the country's highways together and appeared on the same programme at clubs and theatres. Sadly Ronnie passed away recently but he will never be forgotten by countless friends and fans, including yours truly.

I also remember the time when Roy accompanied Harry Ramsden — son of the famous fish fryer — to Blackpool, where they met a peer of the realm. His lordship was friendly. Roy and Harry were on their best behaviour. They sounded their aitches in the right and wrong places and — when the evening drew to a close — the noble lord invited them to his hotel for a nightcap.

'Much as we would like to come, I'm sorry we cannot accept your offer', Harry murmured. 'Any road up — we've left us coats at t' Crown.'

It is a funny expression, isn't it? 'Any road up' is probably peculiar to this part of the world. The derivation is possibly lost in the mists of time.

Any road up — if God spares me, I'll keep scribbling.

Moggy with a Nose for News

Moggy Morgan was my nickname at school, and I have had a love-hate relationship with the feline world ever since. Cats and I do not get on. They spit, hiss and make a habit of sharpening their needle-pointed claws on my ankle bones. I would not hurt one, but I almost have kittens when they pounce uninvited on to my expansive lap to yawn and miaow for attention.

My bachelor pal Bill is different. He is cat crazy, and settles happily in the huge armchair in his basement flat where he nurses and strokes Charlie for hours on end. Charlie hates me and he knows that I am not enamoured with him. But he has at least one loyal fan in addition to his doting owner. Bill discovered recently that someone else — out of sheer kindness — was feeding his pet and Charlie was putting on weight at an alarming rate. Bill tried without success to pinpoint the generous but erring neighbour, and he left a postcard on his front gate with the plea: 'Will the person who has been feeding my cat please stop.' The following day he peered at the card and written underneath Bill's instruction was: 'Sorry, can't stop — in a hurry. PS — I've fed the cat.'

I tell you this story, dear reader, simply because I am an inveterate reader of pamphlets, bulletins, and any sign or notice stuck on a lamp post, wall, window or even windscreen. I am just a nosey parker.

I remember the instruction stuck on the old-fashioned cash registers in Cashdisha, Fosters, Hitchens and even Woolworths, Leeds. It read: 'Cash must be registered before the goods are wrapped.'

I recall peering through one dusty window and attempting to decipher the initials EFFIES, only to realise it was a popular name for St Faith's Home For Fallen Females.

Our local landlord has put up a sign which informs skint customers: 'I have an agreement with the bank manager. He does not sell beer and I do not lend money.'

But the one which always irritates is the curt warning which trespasses under refined politeness. It reads: 'Please do not ask for credit because refusal might offend.'

This spells out in no uncertain terms: 'Do not ask for tick' — a practice which was the 'norm' when I was a kid. You used to see mums doing the weekly shopping and handing over a little red cash book for the proprietor to enter the latest debt in the ever-increasing overdrawn column. The mother would then say 'I'll pay off half-a-crown this week, Mr so-and-so', and blush in front of cash-carrying customers who did not require the facility of 'ticking it up'. They called them the good old days. I wonder if they were.

I only know that the good times are still here for Charlie the cat. He's just nipped me where it hurts most — and I don't mean in the pocket.

Dressing for the Occasion

It's called dressing for the occasion. We all do it. We don our frippery for special events and we parade like peacocks in our best bib and tuckers.

I have worn regulation morning dress twice, and both attempts to 'look like something I ain't' ended in disaster. The first time was at my daughter's wedding, the second when my eldest son plighted his troth.

The decree went out that dress would be formal. Off I trotted to a hire firm and was quite happy with the coat, pants, waistcoat, shirt, cravat and, of course, a crowning topper. I tried everything on but the shirt and stiff collar, and all appeared to fit like the proverbial glove. I also ordered a pair of those just to drape with a touch of nonchalance over the brim of my upturned top hat.

I collected the box of sartorial goodies on the eve of my daughter's marriage and decided that it was unnecessary to have another try-on of the clothing. But I wished that I had done. Half an hour before I was ready to leave for the church I pulled on the pants and, to my horror, they were six inches too long. They had obviously been mixed with another hirer's trousers and, of course, he would be at another 'do' with his bags at half-mast. There was not much I could do at this juncture. The Lovely Maureen tried to turn them up for me but the tacking came loose halfway up the aisle.

And it was not long before I was threatening to trip into a headlong plunge at the feet of the waiting Reverend Father Jackson. He must have thought that the stumbling apparition approaching with the faltering gait had already been at the whisky bottle, and so must the majority of those in the congregation who watched what should have been a proud father pulling at the waistband of his trousers and trying to haul them up round his chest.

But my son's wedding was even worse. We tried on our grey clothes from Moss Bros. I checked that everything was in order. I was in no mood for a repetition of the previous experience. I was determined not to be twice bitten. Two days later I picked up the garments and the family set off in convoy down to Wales for the happy day.

We booked in an hotel and looked forward to the rather splendid reception at the exclusive St Pierre Golf Club because my heir married into a family with a healthier bank balance than I will ever possess. It was a swell affair. It was swish and ritzy. It was a time for showing off. And I would have relished every second but for the clothes.

Believe it or not, but I had been given the wrong box again. Nothing fitted. The coat gripped me under the armpits. The trousers were at half-mast, revealing a generous expanse of socks above my crippling footwear. I was like the man from the Bahamas whose skin-tight pyjamas threatened the welfare of his 'Huntley and Palmers'. The topper was akin to a pea on a drum and the shirt was monstrous. It was at least two sizes too small, and Lord only knows how the Lovely Maureen managed to fasten it round my strangulated neck.

The cravat was attached and I arrived at the service looking like a fugitive from a Hal Roach film. My neck bulged over the constricted collar. I couldn't speak. The voice box was gripped in a vice. I turned salmon pink, cardinal red, and finally purple before the ceremony and eventually the torture came to an end. As the priest intoned the words 'What God hath joined together let no man put asunder', the collar suddenly expelled the stud with the speed of a Scud missile. It brought instant relief. My face eventually turned from puce to pink and I breathed again.

But my troubles were not over. I was accused of showing the family up, and I was warned by embarrassed folk on my side of the gathering — under the pain of mortal punishment — not to appear on the wedding photographs.

I was in savage mood when I returned to the hire shop. I slammed my box on the counter and embarked on a string of complaints with the assistant on the defensive. He had his handkerchief stuffed into his mouth as I described my experience and he murmured from behind suppressed giggles:

'You must have picked up the wrong gear, sir. I can assure you that the original garments tried on by you were the ones we put out for you. There must have been some mistake.'

I tried in vain to get a rebate on the money I had spent. The chap was not in a mood to offer me financial compensation. But he checked over the clothes I had returned. I waited for

my deposit. I was still angry. And I nearly exploded with wrath and indignation when the bloke murmured: 'There is one thing not accounted for sir. Where is the stud? I can't find the stud.'

I grabbed my deposit. I fixed him with a look of outrage. I felt the blood pressure boiling again. That pink salmon hue was returning, and I simply turned on my heel and intended striding from the premises with as much pomposity as I could muster. Unfortunately my pride was once again pricked. I walked smack into the full-length mirror, and grabbed a curtain on one of the changing booths just to steady myself. It fell from its pole and I finished on my knees staring into the face of my hire shop tormentor. I could have cried.

My tale of toppers and tails is told. I will always be reluctant to wear them again. But I suppose it is inevitable that the day will dawn when once again I have to dress for the occasion.

Fire, Brimstone and Good Old Mr Lazarus

Mr Lazarus owned what is termed these days a one-plus-one business. He was the hard-working boss and my mother Norah was the equally industrious employee.

Mr Lazarus and Norah were religious persons. They worshipped the same God — he at the synagogue, and Norah at Mount St Mary's Church where Irish-born priests preached fire and brimstone, and threatened eternal damnation to those errant members of the flock who strayed from the fold.

I remember leaving after one particular service with a quaking heart and troubled soul. Our family attended a fortnight's mission at which visiting preachers thumped the pulpit and predicted blood and thunder for those who transgressed and did not make amends. But after half a dozen consecutive nights of listening to the same theme, one could understand and forgive any little lad for slipping into slumberland while the priest waded into the subject of sin without sorrow and the dire consequences of such a mortal act. The cleric's farewell sentence was delivered with a voice designed to waken the dead. And I almost shot from my skin when he screamed: 'Repent — or you will all burn in Hell like faggots!' I just caught the last few words. I did not hear the proviso of repentance. I fled from the church fully reconciled to the claim that I would end my worldly sojourn in a state of fiery torment.

And for all you and I know, I may end up stoking Old Nick's furnace because I have the necessary credentials. I am fully qualified in such work. It was Mr Lazarus who gave me the experience.

When I was a child, I knew and felt that there were only two major differences in the creeds followed by Mr Lazarus, and by my mother and me. We did not eat meat on Fridays. And Mr Lazarus did not work on Saturdays. We always had fish on the meatless days. And Mr Lazarus refrained from labouring on the Sabbath. That was the one day of the week when he did not sit with his legs crossed, tailoring jackets in his dimly lit shop, and peering with pride through pebble-lensed spectacles at the neat row of hand-stitches he hemmed

in the lapels. This was his trademark. You could always tell a
Mr Lazarus suit by the lapels.

It was Mr Lazarus who introduced me to fires, if not flood
and pestilence. He was also the one who allayed my deeply
held fears about my destiny of damnation. He told me every
Saturday morning, as I raked out the ashes from his fireplace
and stacked the grate with twisted knots of newspaper,
firewood ('chips', we called them) and coal ready for Sunday
lighting:

'You are a good boy, John. And good boys will not come to
harm. Your mother is a good person and good mothers do
not have bad boys.'

His comforting philosophy was all the solace and encouragement I required to give the grate an extra polish. I would
smear on the blacklead. And the brushes would fly like the
proverbial fiddler's elbow to bring the metal surrounds to as
shiny a lustre as one could muster.

Mr Lazarus did not do what he called his 'chores' on
Saturdays. He left them for Norah and me. He was always
quiet as though in a state of contemplation on this special day
of rest. But during the week he was a beaver. He worked all
hours that God sent. He always had a tale to tell. He was a

fount of knowledge and he played his part in nurturing the harmony which existed between the Cohens and the Kellys.

It was Mr Lazarus who suggested that Izzy Bonn and John McCormick should appear in a joint concert at Leeds Town Hall to raise funds required to rebuild a Catholic church which had been destroyed by fire. The renowned artistes were regrettably not available, but the show did proceed with local performers, of different religious persuasions, giving freely of their talents to assist in the erection of a structure which stands today as a living testimony to their togetherness.

I was reminded of Mr Lazarus at the weekend when a priest, of more than his allotted Biblical span, recalled the conversation Father Murphy once had with Rabbi Green. They talked of many things, and they eventually turned to the subject of how to make faith more popular.

Father Murphy declared: 'Your trouble is that you and your priests do not try anything new. You don't evangelise or advertise on television or in newspapers. You do not try to get your message across. The modern world is leaving you behind.'

Rabbi Green waited with infinite patience for Father Murphy to finish his observations and he gently murmured: 'It is quite obvious to me, Father, that you know very little, if anything at all, about our Jewish religion. After all, Samson had this advertising business taped over three thousand years ago. He took two columns and brought down the house!'

Mr Lazarus — and Norah — would have appreciated the story, and also the tale of the young rabbi who noticed that an elderly member of his congregation always fell asleep just as he started his sermon. But at the end of the service, the old man was always enthusiastic in praise of the eulogy. It happened every week, and one day the youthful preacher simply had to say:

'I'm sure you will not mind me mentioning this, but I notice you always sleep through my sermons. So how come you always thank me for what I have said?

'Look at it this way', the wise worshipper smiled. 'If I didn't trust you, how could I sleep?'

I think I have also wakened up at long last. I can't believe that I will burn in hell like faggots. Mr Lazarus gave me his word that I wouldn't. And that will do for me.

Old Snecklifters and New Beggars

The first time I heard the expression 'snecklifter' was outside the pub in the yard at the back of the City Varieties, Leeds. The hostelry has had several names. At that time it was known as the Piccadilly Bar and frequented by characters that might have stepped out of a Damon Runyon saga. I remember Corny Mac, Chicken Joe, Anthony 'Ascot' Heath, Diamond Jack, Clicky Hoban, Alan Blackjack, Jonas Bletherbottom (honest) and many more who contributed to the colourful city scene.

It was there a chap waited at the bottom of the stairs leading to the betting shop, owned by Milky Marks. And he shuffled over with palm outstretched. He gazed through soulful eyes and pleaded: 'Can you give me a snecklifter because I need a cheeker-in, my old tatey.' I can assure you that I was not even his new potato — never mind one of long standing. But I pressed a bob into his grateful fist and he beat me to the pumps in the Piccadilly Bar.

Years ago, most back-to-back houses had a front door with a round glass knob. But the back door had a metal 'sneck' which was pressed down. This lifted the latch so that members of the family, visitors, and even bailiffs, could gain entrance. The 'snecklifter' or 'cheeker-in' was also the price of a drink which enabled a skint drinker to enter the pub. He would then stand on the fringe of assembled imbibers in the hope that he would be included in the rounds.

I thought of 'my old tatey' the other day when I was stopped four times by hard-up folk on a walk round the shopping precinct. But perhaps advancing years have sapped my generosity. I don't think I am as gullible as I used to be. And although the tragic plight of homeless youngsters tugs at the heart strings, I am ashamed to admit that I often steel my feelings against many other pleading approaches.

I am suspicious of a young fellow who sits at the side of a notice on which is scrawled: 'Homeless — and hungry. Please help.' He is on shift work. When he breaks for a fag, one of his pals takes over the site and adopts a baleful countenance born out of practice. This image of destitute misery disappears when his colleague returns to take over the squat.

One of my greatest friends was born into abject poverty. He was one of six children and said: 'I never knew what it was to sleep alone until I got married.' He left school and made good in business. But the recession has taken its toll and he complained: 'Things are so bad that even customers with no intention of paying have stopped ordering.' He added: 'I will be out on the streets before long.' And I might even join him.

Having a Go with Wilfred

It was that bubbling broadcaster Kathryn Apanovicz who turned my thoughts to the late Wilfred Pickles when she asked me to take part in her radio show *Have a Go*.

No doubt she wanted me to recall the days of Wilfred and his wife Mabel, and trot out one or two anecdotes about the Yorkshireman who enjoyed a career as shop assistant, newsreader, actor, quizmaster, pantomime star and poet. But no!

I arrived in the studio for the live interview and perched before effervescent Kathryn with my favourite recollections of Wilfred ready to burst on the unsuspecting listeners. At times like this I try to portray a cool exterior, although the mere presence of a microphone is sufficient to give me butterflies, hence the torrent of words which gush and gain momentum as my contribution hits the airwaves. So you can imagine the inner panic when Kathryn told me she was asking me to 'Have A Go' and answer such soul-searching questions as 'When did you have your first kiss?', followed by 'Name your favourite schoolteacher'.

I had to confess to the adorable Kathryn — a gal with an infectious giggle — that to my eternal shame I was not aware of the content of her programme and that we had got our wireless wires crossed. But at least I was able to tell her of the original *Have a Go* programme, which lasted for two decades, travelled the length and breadth of the British Isles and had regular audiences of more than 20 million listeners. It was unscripted and off the cuff. It was homespun fun and visited hamlets, villages, towns, and cities where inhabitants were invited on stage in front of fans, family and friends to answer innocent questions. It was mostly predictable, but we all waited for the moment when Wilfred introduced that incisive query which drew crimson blushes from embarrassed and probably spotty teenagers: 'Are you courting?' This was sufficient to stir the locals into gales of laughter as the 'victim' shuffled and stumbled.

But there is one question that I will never forget because it resulted in a major change in *Have a Go*'s format. Wilfred was on stage with a genteel old lady of four score years, and she faithfully answered his queries about the neighbourhood local customs, and the rest. He finally produced his poser: 'If you could make the world a happier place in which to live, what would you do?' The pert pensioner replied: 'I would buy everyone a bicycle and we would ride round the streets — smiling at each other.' Wilfred, with due solemnity, murmured: 'What a beautiful thought!' And the audience erupted into a burst of applause. Wilfred then turned to producer Barney Colehan and whispered: 'Have you ever heard such bloody nonsense?' Unfortunately this *sotto voce* aside was heard by millions and the expletive shocked the nation. Wilfred was summoned to appear before the broadcasting hierarchy and censured. *Have a Go* had been a live programme up to Wilfred's slip of the tongue. After that it was recorded and subjected to editing before it was allowed to burst into our living room from the domed Cossor radio.

Barney Colehan was a good friend. We enjoyed many a happy chat, and his flying-officer handlebar moustache fairly bristled when he talked of his triumphs with the universally acclaimed *Good Old Days* at Leeds City Varieties. His pink features always creased into a smile when he reflected on *Have a Go* and the estimated half-million miles he and the team travelled to mount the broadcast.

One of the ever-presents on the show was Violet Carson, who played the piano as volunteers walked on and off stage. She also thumped out the signature tune which the audience sang, although I can't remember anything but the opening lines which went: 'Have a go Joe, come on and have a go ...' Violet progressed to play Ena Sharples in *Coronation Street*.

Wilfred's wife Mabel was another key figure. She maintained a check on a simple competition which resulted in half-crowns and two-bob pieces making a jackpot prize for the end of the broadcast. 'How much money on the table, Mabel?' asked Wilfred. 'Twenty-two shillings and sixpence' was typical of her reply, and the first contestant to shout out the solution to a most trivial question walked off with the cash and other items donated by members of the audience. It was clean and uncomplicated entertainment. It was neither cynical or sophisticated, and its success was its simplicity.

Wilfred was born in Halifax and always proud of his Yorkshire roots. He worked in the family business with his father, who was a builder, and he dabbled in amateur dramatics. He secured a job with the BBC reading the news although his northern accent did not suit every listener. Wilfred first hit the headlines when he ended one news summary with 'good night and to all northerners wherever you are, good neet'. This caused a furore, but Wilfred was allowed to repeat his 'neet' on not a few occasions. I first met him when he was in pantomime at the Theatre Royal, Leeds, and remember another long conversation with him and Mabel in the General Wade Bar at the Merrion Hotel, Leeds. I recall that with clarity because thrifty Wilfred did not pay for a drink all night but kept us entertained with stories — true and otherwise. He certainly had the gift of the gab and he enjoyed a giggle — like Kathryn Apanovicz.

The Busy Bees Next Door

Charlie and Peggy were ideal neighbours. They didn't borrow cups of sugar. But they were fond of our children, kind to our assortment of animals, and, when Charlie trimmed his neat privet hedge, he always clipped my wilderness before cleaning and stowing away the shears.

But the devoted couple did have one fault. They were ultra-house proud. Peggy never stopped whipping round the happy homestead with her whirring Hoover, and she was just as incessant with the flicking of her feather duster. Charlie was also a busy bee. He was restless when he was idle. Peggy almost had to fasten the manacles to stop him painting his woodwork and changing the wallpaper at least once a month.

We always knew when another session of decorating was on the launching pad. Charlie used to whistle a tuneless tune. He would spit on his hands, open his garden shed door, pull out a step-ladder and pasting table, and hurtle into fast and furious slap-dash action. He would not be seen for three or four days, and we would sit in our totally lived-in house and wait for the urgent summons to inspect his handiwork.

'Come in and have a cup of tea', invited Charlie, and he would suck on his pipe, puff out his chest and stand with increasing anticipation for our gushing words of admiration. I used to keep him waiting. I would sip my tea, nibble my Garibaldi and pretend that I hadn't noticed a change in the colour scheme, even though a room which was pastel pink yesterday was now a shocking orange. Charlie used to get impatient. He would rock on his heels and then point the stem of his pipe at the newly-covered walls before demanding: 'What do you think then? Do you notice owt different? I bet you can't find a joining.'

And that was the signal for us to go overboard with lavish praise of his DIY expertise. The Lovely Maureen would describe him as 'an artist' and 'a one-off'. And she would glance in my direction and add: 'I only wish other people were as industrious.'

But my spouse — and Peggy — changed their minds about Charlie's handiwork when he moved into the 'contact' age.

The fabric was like oilcloth with a backing paper. You peeled this off to reveal a sticky surface, and simply stretched it across anything you wanted to cover. You could wipe it clean, and it certainly made a more serviceable and more hygienic table-cloth than a spread-out copy of the evening paper.

But it became a problem for Charlie. He was obsessed with the stuff. He bought rolls of it in all colours. And he stretched it on all objects — movable and otherwise. He applied a purple-quilted variety on his bed headboard. He plastered it on every door. The interior of his trim semi-detached dwelling was well and truly stuck-up. Even the toilet seat was covered with the thick-bubbled type of material — giving all who entered the tiny room the feeling that they had been admitted to a padded cell. It was attached to the cistern, light-switches, the washing machine and fridge. Charlie spread it on pelmets, stools, cabinets, the surrounds near the sink, and window sills. And Peggy feared that if she stood still long enough, she would be covered from head to toe with a rather nice line in floral design. It was all over the place. Charlie 'papered' the walls of his shed with 'contact'. He even wound it round the handles of his fork, spade and shears. And the stick-on craze lasted for months, until Charlie discovered an alternative.

He fell for red-flock wallpaper — the sort used as decor in old-type musical halls and still in evidence in dimly-lit Indian restaurants of my patronage. The flock bristled with diamond designs. And Charlie was lavish in his use of it without entirely discarding 'contact'.

But the time came when Charlie and Peggy had to reluctantly depart from our district, and we inherited — for a few pounds — his almost new and delightful comfortable double-bed with its monstrosity of a stuck-on quilted head-board. It gave me nightmares.

Charlie and Peggy sold their semi to a young couple whose taste in decor was definitely on a higher plane. And they tackled the job of restoration with more energy than I ever possessed. They stripped the walls with enthusiastic vigour, and discovered eight layers of wallpaper of different hues and texture hiding under the red-flocked eyesore. They almost pulled the skirting board from its base in a futile attempt to separate it from its 'contact' covering. As for the 'lavvy' seat, it finished up on the dustcart with the padded pelmets.

I often think of Charlie and Peggy. And learned that sadly they are no longer with us. They will probably be helping the angels to decorate some celestial abode.

Open All Hours

Lord only knows what the EC, with its regulations and restrictions, would have made of our old-time corner shops. They were not only 'open all hours' for the sale of commodities but provided a meeting place for shopping housewives to have a good chinwag.

It was not a case of serve yourself, pack your trolley and pay at the checkout. Individual attention was the keynote, with the shopkeeper — on first-name terms with the majority of his customers — serving those at the head of the queue as gossiping ladies waited patiently for their turn.

The European sticklers for hygiene would have had a field day with our Mr Woodhead & Sons — a real family firm. He had 'General Provision Merchant' painted on a sign above the window, which was always covered with whitewashed lettering proclaiming everything to be 'freshly picked, freshly caught and freshly wrapped'.

Sugar was in huge open sacks, with a scoop handy to feed the sweet contents into stiff blue paper bags. Butter was uncovered in a huge mound with wooden spatulas to pat the creamy slabs into the required weight. Hams hung from ceiling hooks above a huge cheese which was sliced into portions with a wire. There was one case with polonies, penny ducks, sausages, black puddings, bacon joints ready for the slicer, meat pies of all sizes and huge jars of pickles.

There were well-filled flypapers curling from the roof with insects adhering to the sticky surfaces. There was always a distinct odour of paraffin, coal bricks, firelighters, and firewood with loops of wire holding the bundles of sticks together. There was sawdust on the floor, and clouds of dust rose at the end of the day when the premises were swept by Mr Woodhead & Sons.

EC inspectors would have had a dicky fit. But we were probably immune to corner shop germs. Outbreaks of dysentery or tummy trouble were usually attributed to smelly 'fever' grates — especially in summer when the aroma was its most pungent.

We did, however, have 'spotless' shops, with the likes of Liptons, Gallons, Maypole and the Thrift Stores as clean as

the proverbial whistle. They were the forerunners of today's supermarkets, with counter staff in Rinso white coats. Smart ladies tucked their hair in snoods, and tongs were employed to lift slices of Spam or Prem on to the scales.

Our local Co-operative grocery store had a butchery department attached in the pre-EC days, when beef was safe and pork chops could be bought with kidneys attached.

Frank Wilson worked there, and he never tired of telling the story of a lady who asked him if he had any bones for the dog. Frank wrapped up a pile and the customer queried the price. Frank replied: 'You can have them for nothing.' The shopper bristled and snapped: 'I'm not standing for that — you are not doing me out of my divi.'

We were a Co-op family. We needed the 'divi'. But I will never forget our corner shop and its open tin of biscuits for kiddies to stick in their grubby hands and take the stipulated 'only one for each child'. And I'll never forget the sawdust either ...

Tales of the Dark Ages

Over fifty-five years ago, Britain emerged from a cloak of darkness. The blackout, officially declared on the 1st September 1939, was lifted at 9.30pm on the 24th April 1945.

Drawn curtains were parted and light streamed from windows. Disbelieving citizens — cautious at first — stood in silent awe. Slowly but surely the truth dawned. For the first time in 2,062 nights, there was no diligent air-raid warden to bark: 'Put that light out.' Houses shone like beacons. People blinked at the unfamiliar illumination. Such was the intensity of the 'switch-on' that isolated power failures occurred.

But this time the blackout was short-lived, unlike the one which descended as a pall of gloom and signalled the outbreak of war. The real blackout was a dismal experience, and added to the bewilderment of travellers who also had to contend with missing road signs. Street names disappeared as part of the plan to baffle invaders. Drivers often came to a full stop at unmarked crossroads, and based the rest of their journey on luck and guesswork.

We covered our windows with black cardboard pinned on a wooden frame. This was put up every night and taken down the following morning until it disintegrated. Many criss-crossed window panes with brown sticky paper to prevent flying glass from bomb blasts. We didn't follow that precaution, but dutifully pulled the curtains tight and prevented even a chink of light from our low-watt bulb incurring the ire of our watchful warden.

We ventured out at night with the aid of a tiny torch. The beam was muffled by a couple of layers of tissue paper. Many tales were told of collisions with strangers, chaps bumping into lamp posts and apologising, courting couples being caught in the dim glow of the flashlight, and folk taking the wrong turnings.

But the streets seemed to be safer in those dark days than they are now. The danger came from the skies and not from muggers, although I recall unwittingly striking panic into a lady who clip-clopped on high heels in front of me. It was pitch black — not a star in the sky — and I suddenly had an

urge to cough. I did, and the girl screamed blue murder and fled. Honestly, I was more scared than her.

There was laughter in wartime despite the hostilities, austerity and the darkness. And there was joy, elation and eager anticipation on the night the blackout order was rescinded. The 24th April 1945 brought light and life back to Britain — and the world at large.

The Last Resort

Have you planned your holidays? Have you a mixed collection of glossy brochures spread over the front room carpet? Will you be spending the summer vacation abroad, or will you be backing Britain and making Blackpool, Bognor or Bridlington your last resort?

I ask you this because I have a date in Blackpool and will be at the famed Winter Gardens — home to many a political conference. But this time several thousand pigeons will be on stage for the fluttering admiration of fanciers of this popular breed. No doubt their billing and cooing will make more sense than all the hot air spouted at those Tory and Labour party meetings. And I am looking forward to the trip if only because I haven't walked in the shadow of Blackpool Tower for the proverbial yonks.

Time was when Blackpool was a tiny fishing village with fewer than a thousand inhabitants. But the advent of railway transport gave Lancashire and Yorkshire folk the chance to visit such places. And it was not long before Blackpool became a firm favourite with people from the right and wrong side of the Pennines.

The town is now home to 150,000 residents. It attracts eight million visitors each summer, and even the most cynical Yorkshireman will reluctantly admit that the place is one of the largest and most spectacular holiday centres in Europe.

My father was as fiercely proud of his birthright as any son of the Broad Acres. But he was loyal to Blackpool. He never went anywhere else and, when it came to choosing the venue for our family holiday, it was a one-horse race. Blackpool came first and the rest were also-rans.

He saved up all the year round to pay the bill at Miss Pickin's lodgings in Withnell Road, South Shore — at the side of the Pleasure Beach — and the digs were so posh they had a residents' lounge, with the biggest aspidistra in the world; an upright piano, with the lid firmly locked; antimacassars on the back of the horsehair chairs and sofa; and cheese and biscuits for supper if you returned to the premises before 9pm.

Miss Pickin's father, who was all trousers and braces, used to heave his brewer's belly on to the front gate, and peer

down Withnell Road through a set of ancient binoculars. They were the type you could rent in the theatre, but strong enough for him to pick out visitors who were in danger of being thirty seconds late for lunch or not galloping — as requested — to the evening meal. Mr Pickin always greeted you with: 'Punctuality is a virtue. I insist on folk being punctual. I don't agree with keeping a meal waiting.'

At the end of the fortnight, our grateful father invariably wrote in the visitors' book: 'Home from Home'. But we had to be nudged by our doting dad to nod our heads in response to the annual threat from Miss Pickin: 'See you next year.'

The aim in those far-off days was for all holidaymakers to increase their weight. If you didn't return home a stone heavier than when you arrived at the seaside, you had not fulfilled the principal intention. Miss Pickin served lashings of cholesterol and calories. And we were encouraged to scoff the lot, clean our plates and eat the burnt bits because, we were assured, such morsels gave you curly hair. Have you ever heard such nonsense? But we believed every word.

Blackpool hasn't towered over me for years. Perhaps snobbery arrived with senility. I have wandered the world in search of more exotic spots since my childhood hols. But I must admit that I am looking forward to my visit — the golden sands, empty promenade, screaming seagulls, and even those thousands of pigeons.

Sweet and Spicy Memories

Why do Yorkshire folk call sweets 'spice'? It seems a contradiction in terms, although my schoolboy adventure stories often mentioned 'the ships from faraway places laden with gold, silks, and sweet spices from the Orient'.

My great-aunt Lizzie — the one who sold trunnel pies and mushy peas in Leeds market — also had a sweet shop on the Bank, which was often affectionately referred to in rhyming slang as 'the Hamshank'.

If we adhere to my old mother's saying 'tell the truth and shame the devil', we will admit that the Bank was a gigantic slum. The area suffered from mortal decay. But we had our sweet shops, and none more popular than great Aunt Lizzie's humble front room which had a counter packed with jars of bull's-eyes and other bonbons.

There was another shop that sold nothing but brittle slabs of tooth-threatening toffee. But Lizzie had a wider selection of goodies. It was a veritable paradise of 'spice' on which children splashed their weekly penny.

This was a happy task, but one not taken lightly. You pressed your face at the window — like the Bisto Kids — and silently surveyed the boxes of tempting sweeties before making a selection. A penny would stretch to a couple of ounces of mixed sweets or even a Lucky Bag if you were prepared to take pot luck with your purchase. You can imagine how many sweets or spice one could buy at Whitsuntide when extra pennies were given to children who paraded in their 'Whitsy' finery for admiring relatives.

It was in the early 1930s when slum clearance saw the demolition of the Bank — the end of Lizzie's shop — and a new life for those transported from muck and rubble to housing estates like Gipton, Seacroft and Halton Moor. It was an exciting era, but little did we know in the mid-1930s that Adolf Hitler was preparing to plunge the world into another terrible period of wartime hostilities. Our contented days of unlimited sweets at posh shops like Mittons in Easterly Road, Whelans on Brander Road, Jack Craig's at the top of Gipton Approach, and Granelli's in Hudson Road, near Burton's vast tailoring factory, were numbered.

Rationing was in the pipeline. We were about to be introduced to years of austerity, and a savage reduction in the quantity and variety of sweets or spice. Sweets were available on 'personal points', and I can still remember squandering my monthly allowance on a slab of bitter unsweetened plain chocolate which almost cracked your molars.

However, before and after the ravages and harsh deprivation of the long and unhappy war years, we had sweets galore if you could afford them. Do you recall Love Hearts, gob-stoppers, Sherbet Dabs, Hazelnut Creams, Clarnico Chocolate Creams, Snowballs, Palm Toffee Kali, Buttered Brazils and those funny-tasting Locust Beans? Do you remember long strips of chewy toffee, creamy fudge, marzipan teacakes, monkey nuts and sweets which resembled potatoes, peas and carrots?

They certainly spiced up our post-war days.

Hair Today and None Tomorrow

They called it Morgans Pomade. It was a hairdressing concoction elderly gentlemen applied to their greying locks, and I am toying with the idea of getting some now that my once light-brown crowning glory is streaked with silver.

I first spotted Morgans Pomade when I was a callow youth — earning fifteen shillings a week, including a twenty-five per cent war bonus. And in those days I scoured Leeds for the cheapest haircut and eventually became a regular customer at the barber's shop in Leed's market. It was not exactly a tonsorial emporium. It was not the most salubrious salon. It was, in fact, positioned in a corner of the gentlemen's urinal, and down the steps from Rileys, where one could purchase sheet music, second-hand ukeleles, and those push-button melodeons beloved of seafaring folk.

One of the barbers was a tall ginger-headed gentleman, who walked with a limp. And I recall him recommending Morgans Pomade to one client and my ears immediately quivered at the mention of my name.

I did fall for one hairdressing aid — it was a green solidified brilliantine. It had the consistency of the kaolin your mother spread on a poultice and slapped on your chest. It used to sting my uncultured nostrils into twitching appreciation of the fragrance. But one sniff was sufficient to send more discerning people dashing for their gas mask.

The tall barber — with the limp — used to spread it on my curls, rub it in until the scalp tingled, and then he would get to work with two brushes. Hair was dragged back from the temple and simply plastered down. And this youth — who entered the premises with a mass of soft waving curls — always emerged with glistening straight hair brushed in the style of the film-star gangster George Raft.

An increase in salary saw me switch my hair-dressing patronage to Bensons in Albion Place, Leeds, and my initial visit was not without fright. It was there I first saw singeing taking place, and sat with mouth agape as the barber passed a lighted taper over the customer's hair, setting it on fire, and immediately combing out the flames. This, I learned, was a method of sealing the ends of the hair, strengthened the

growth, and prevented influenza germs from dashing down the roots, into the head, and then into the chest, lungs and, wherever such bugs are prone to visit.

It was also where I first saw barbers dig into an aluminium container with tongs and pull out a steaming hot towel which they wafted from one hand to another before dropping it on the face of a chap in the chair. He sat with only his nostrils visible. His cheeks turned crimson as the barber patted what looked like a boiling flannel, and how he stood it only the good Lord will ever know. I would have hit the roof along with the vapours which soared to the ceiling.

Lathering, stropping cut-throat razors on leather straps hanging from a specially designed chair, stiptic pencils to stop bleeding, and bottles upon bottles of various creams were seen in all the barbers' shops.

And, of course, grown men used to discreetly whisper in the ear of the chap who had just cut their hair and money would surreptitiously change hands. And an equally secretive exchange of goods would be made and quickly rammed into the buyer's pocket. I thought that the barber was selling racing tips but years later I learned that this was not the case.

I had to switch from Bensons because our general manager started to use the place, and one mid-afternoon he found one of the employees having his hair trimmed. 'You should have your hair cut in your own hours', the boss growled. He did not take kindly to the lad's excuse: 'Well, it grows in the firm's time, sir.'

To avoid a similar confrontation I took my custom to Mick Homburg's — nearly opposite the Corn Exchange, and just a few yards down from Hayes shellfish shop where you could buy a bag of crab claws. It was in Mick's that I sat next to a man who was known in the area as Gerry Dorsey and eventually found fame as Engelbert Humperdinck. His haircut seemed to take hours and it always looked as long when he left as it was when he entered. It's nice to know he's done so well.

But ladies in those far-off days also had a different carry-on with the weekly hair-do. They timed it so that they were perfectly coiffured for their Saturday night dates with George Raft or Tommy Lawton look-alikes. And I can still picture lasses tying rags in their tresses, sleeping in them, and when they untied them the hair would drop in ringlets. Then came the evil-smelling home perms which had all the odour of bad eggs. One solution was applied and the hair wound tightly round grips. Then the second solution was put on — all in the painful pursuit of vanity. But I suppose they were safer than curling tongs which were heated in coal fires and applied to damp hair which they crimped with a frightening hiss. They were nearly as lethal as those towels which turned pale gents into panting and pained examples of purple-faced purity.

Barbers, of course, were once blood-letters and appliers of blood-sucking leeches. But nowadays they are tonsorial artistes with nifty scissor-work, expensive shampoos, costly conditioners and services never even dreamed of in my formative years. But I wonder if they have any Morgans Pomade? I could do with a ton of the stuff.

Tanks for the Memory

Kaiser Wilhelm and Adolf Hitler failed to halt production of munitions and tanks at Barnbow's historic Royal Ordnance Factory (ROF) in two world wars. But the combined forces of owners Vickers, the government, and the ever-prevalent and iniquitous threat of redundancies closed the firm, adding 700 justifiably angry workers to the unemployed list.

My mother was 'on munitions' at Barnbow in the First World War and suffered from a virulent outbreak of an affliction described as 'TNT poisoning'. Many young ladies with the task of filling shells for big guns were victims of the persistent malady for which they had little or no protective clothing. It was a type of jaundice, a yellow peril, which did nothing to enhance the sufferer's complexion, hair lustre or general health.

The workers not only despatched loaded ammunition to the battle grounds. They also sent good luck cards, knitted woollies, scarves, caps and other little comforts to the 'Tommies' locked in bloody warfare. My mother volunteered for service as a tram conductress in 1915. But she was termed 'too young', although there was no age bar to teenagers labouring at Barnbow.

When the Second World War — hopefully the last — flared into tragic and frightening hostility, employment at Barnbow and other ROF sites soared. Men unable to pass medical examinations for entry into the army, navy or air force opted for work in the munitions factories. Many were recruited for Barnbow, which also utilised the hitherto unknown skills and industry of girls who wore dungarees and neatly-tied head-squares, which caught on as an unofficial uniform. Girls became proficient at jobs believed to be the preserve of the male gender, and at least one ditty was written and sung about the switch. It went: 'She's the girl that makes the thing that drills the hole that holds the spring, that drives the rod that turns the knob that works the thingumebob.'

These ladies were a vital part of the war effort, and they responded to Winston Churchill's plea on the home front and abroad to 'Give us the tools and we'll finish the job'. Munitions workers, and tank and aeroplane builders listened

to Churchill's inspiring speeches and learned that 'The Front Line runs through the factories', and the cigar-smoking prime minister added: 'Those who work in the factories are soldiers with different weapons but with the same courage.'

Churchill had a type of tank named after him, and we youngsters sacrificed the railings surrounding our park and football pitch to be turned into molten metal and used to manufacture armoured vehicles. Although the absence of the railings made access to the recreational area a simple process, the local park ranger insisted on locking the gates at 8pm each evening to comply with the bye-laws.

It was a strange time in our history. We were told that 'Careless talk costs lives'. And we were urged to 'Be like dad and keep mum'. We also existed on a spartan diet including the famous Woolton Pie, snoek, spam, whale meat and dried egg. Woolton Pie was diced potatoes, cauliflower, swede, carrots, onions and oatmeal under a pastry crust, and it was named after Lord Woolton, the Minister of Food, and a member of the family which owned Lewis's Leeds store.

Churchill promised the Barnbow lasses and lads, every serving man and woman, and every civilian young and old, nothing more than 'Blood, toil, tears and sweat'. He kept his word, and years of austerity followed his edict as munitions workers at Barnbow, and factories in Coventry and Birmingham perspired in their endeavours to produce the essential armaments for our gallant forces.

But there were light relief and musical moments as tanks and jeeps rolled off the assembly belt. *Workers' Playtime* was a daily radio programme, and so was *Music While You Work* which was piped through loudspeakers to war-sickened employees. 'Calling all the factory workers 'cos we know that you're not shirkers' was the signature tune introducing the morning entertainment. *Workers' Playtime* toured munitions works and tailoring firms engaged in the production of uniforms, and the live shows — broadcast on BBC radio — were staged in canteens during the lunch break.

My rare visits to Barnbow were associated with music and dancing. The canteen was regularly used as a dance hall and Ivy Benson and her All-Girl Band played there on the night me and my pals were invited to demonstrate our fox-trot expertise. That occasion was after the war days, which were grim for all concerned — young and old alike. TNT poisoning was not a threat to health in the second encounter with Germany. But deprivation, shortage of food, power cuts, air raids and demanding work had a debilitating effect on morale. There must have been times when the Barnbow employees must have wished and prayed for a quick end to the conflict and a return to a normal family routine.

More recently, the working staff at the time-honoured firm did not ask for the closure of the base and an imminent place in the dole queue. Meanwhile, we who recall Barnbow in wartime with respect and gratitude can only say 'Tanks — for the memory!'

Such Devoted Sisters

My chum Paddy will readily agree that he is partial to a drop of the hard stuff. Two drops are even better. He appreciates a nip of fiery Irish whiskey, and he also renders lip-smacking service to the black-as-ink beverage beloved of boyos from the Emerald Isle.

Paddy is a character. He loves his weekends. And the three 'b's — Bible, beer and bed — dominate the Sabbath, when the red-faced mountain of jollity swaps clay-scuffed boots, overalls and donkey jacket for patent-polished shoes, smart flannels and tailored blazer.

Paddy can be a bit of a toff when he sets out his sartorial stall, and he certainly looked every inch the gentleman when he attended a typical Irish wedding — and a very typical Irish reception. Champagne corks popped. The ale, stout and porter flowed like Dublin's famous Liffey. And Paddy needed no second invitation to help himself.

Paddy had a distinct list to starboard, and his ever-supportive mate Eamonn adopted a similar leaning towards port when they left the flapping sides of the hospitality tent for a much-needed breath of fresh air. The friends linked arms, and they strolled past the local church and meandered down the pavement which skirted the convent.

Out walked two good sisters with whiter-than-white wimples peeping from billowing black headcovers. Rosary beads dangled from leather belts and polished toecaps were visible at the bottom of their ground-brushing skirts. The sisters headed for the brothers-in-beer. Ever-respectful Paddy and Eamonn squinted in the evening haze. They touched their forelocks in salute as the nuns drew near. And the unsteady gait of the revellers must have given a broad hint to the sisters that this was a situation to be avoided with the minimum of small talk.

The men came to a standstill. The nuns separated. One walked round to the left of the duo and the other went to the right. Paddy rubbed his bleary eyes with disbelief and turned to Eamonn with the cry of bewildered astonishment: 'Mother in heaven. How on earth did SHE do that!' It was enough to send them scurrying to sign the pledge.

But they decided that a return to the comfort of the well-stocked bar in the marquee was an infinitely better idea. And Paddy quickly erased memories of the sobering experience when a chap produced a drop of potheen — a spirit guaranteed to strip the enamel from your teeth, curl your toenails, and defer for eternity any decision to desert the demon drink.

We talked about sisters who have played a prominent role in my life, although you don't always recognise nuns — by their garb — these days.

I remember a story, told in those far-off days, of the man who sought shelter in a hostelry. He had his car keys in his hand. He was as white as a sheet and he ordered 'A large Scotch, and quickly please'. He was obviously in a state of shock. He knocked back the drink and gasped: 'How tall are penguins?'

'About two foot I think', the landlord replied.

The chap slapped his hand to his furrowed brow and moaned: 'Dear, oh dear, oh dear. I must have knocked down a nun!'

But times have changed, and so have the sisters' mode of dress, which reminds me of the tale of the two nuns who

drove in their tiny car to a quiet restaurant. The driver parked the car and the sisters entered the cafe to order a pot of tea for two and a couple of cakes. They enjoyed the snack and took their leave. But one sister had inadvertently left her gloves on her chair. The kindly restaurateur picked them up and ran outside, but the nuns had driven away.

He looked in vain for the vehicle and he asked a pedestrian: 'Have you seen a nun in a Mini?'

'No, I haven't', the perplexed fellow replied. 'But I'm not surprised at anything they wear these days.'

Nuns have played an important role in my life.

Sister Philips was one who taught at least ninety-nine per cent of the children who first saw the light of day in the shadow of Mount St Mary's School, near Richmond Hill, Leeds. She was a kindly and much-loved lady. She was caring and gentle. And so concerned about her babes that, when I was in her infants' class, she used to warm our morning milk by standing the bottles round a guard which surrounded the coke fire. Goodness knows what bacteria her lukewarm milk produced. But it was done with good intention, and we never bothered or even knew about germs, bugs and viruses, in those contented days.

I don't hang back when I express my admiration and love for the gracious, industrious, charitable and affectionate nuns I know and respect.

There is one I will always remember. I jived with a slip of a girl at a parochial hop. She was a veritable bundle of rhythmic agility and unrestrained fun. Her face was a picture of radiant joy. And the morning after the dance, she entered a convent.

She is even more joyous and content as a nun, and many of us think of this girl with gratitude. We are thankful that we knew a lass who enriched our lives.

A Spring in my Step

The shock-horror news that the very last waltz would be played at Altmans Ballroom, Leeds, took the spring out of my patent-leather dancing shoes. I quickstepped to the Lovely Maureen to tell her that yet another nostalgic testimony to our happy teenage days had fallen to the unromantic whims of the city planners.

I remember Mark Altman, who taught pupils to move with the grace and elegance of Fred Astaire and Ginger Rogers. I was more like Red Adair attempting to stamp out a fire. But Mark — the maestro — was more successful with the majority of his students who waltzed, slow fox-trotted, and learned pose and posture at his famous dancing academy.

But it was lord help those who preferred the tangle to the tango. I remember a young buck holding his frail lady in a clasp not recognised or countenanced by devotees of strict tempo. Such a passionate embrace was frowned on, and Mark put an immediate stop to the gallivanting. He tapped him on the shoulder and doused the lad's ardour with a thunderous remark: 'Stop that. You come here to dance. Not to make love!' The blushing youth and his equally crimson partner tiptoed from the room with dozens of scandalised eyes following the disgraceful exit. The couple were not seen on the premises for months after the abrupt departure.

I remember dancing at the Mecca Locarno, Leeds, where Ray Ellington and his renowned trio were resident, and where Marian Ryan — mother of the Ryan Twins — was vocalist. I recall Sir James Savile — then plain Jimmy, with tartan-coloured hair — managing that emporium of music and movement.

But Altman's had a special place in our hearts, and always will have. In fact it ranks in my affection with the Colin Hall, on the Sutton Estate, where the rhythm was provided by Eve and the Boys. We also danced with glee at St Nicholas's Parochial Hall with drummer Tony Mazza wielding sticks and brushes and leading his White Knights into sets of dances. After three or four numbers, Tony whispered into the microphone: 'That's all this time please.' And he and his

fellow musicians were refreshed with pints of ale brought in jugs from the Courtier.

Victor Sylvester was the king when it came to pom-pomming strict tempo music, with two pianos giving his orchestra the distinctive sound appreciated throughout the dancing universe. We quickstepped — fishtailed — and did the most intricate footwork to his slow, slow, quick, quick, slow. Victor certainly knew the beat from start to finish, having been world-champion ballroom dancer even before the days of Sally Brock and Sonny Binnick.

I will not play another Victor Sylvester record or another Edmundo Ros disc without thinking of Mark Altman. I will never listen to Woody Herman, Joe Loss, or play the Best of Ivy Benson without remembering those twinkle-toed Saturday afternoons. Neither will I forget being asked to vacate the ballroom. I still turn red when I recall Mark's dismissive: 'Please leave'.

Fiery Fred's Gentle Delivery

Fred Trueman was described by Harold Wilson as the world's greatest living Yorkshireman, and the once fiery fast bowler would be the last to argue with the eminent politician's vehement claim.

Many bless the day he was born in the pit village of Maltby, Rotherham, not the least a flock of after-dinner speakers, who regale listeners with Trueman tales and inform any doubters that the stories are absolutely 'true man'. One or two talkers would not have a speech if it were not for the exploits of Fiery Fred. But he expresses a chuckling denial about the authenticity of many tales of his so-called swashbuckling, hard-living, drink-swilling days with Yorkshire and England.

Fred would not be with us today if half the oft-quoted experiences and incidents had happened. Many of the yarns are apocryphal, and Fred is a much quieter and gentler person than his rough, gruff and tough public image would suggest. Yes, there is a soft side to the man, who hurtled into furious action against the 'enemy' and struck trembling fear into even the most intrepid and talented batsmen.

I'll give you an example of his concern for others. When the cricketing world of Yorkshire spinner Geoff Cope collapsed with allegations of a suspect action, the heart-broken bowler was hounded by the media. They threatened to make life decidedly uncomfortable for Geoff. But the reporters searched for him in vain. It was Fred who sized up the situation. His heart went out to the young cricketer. He collared the distraught sportsman and sheltered him at his lovely Dales cottage until the hue and cry had died. Fred then helped Geoff to re-build his career with advice and encouragement.

Fred has an impish sense of humour. And he bridled when an Australian boasted about the superiority of the Aussies over whingeing poms. Fred readily agreed and added: 'Of course your ancestors were sent here by the best English judges.' Fred greeted incoming Aussie batsmen with a scowl, a whispered warning of 'Don't shut the gate, lad, you won't be long', and usually an unplayable yorker or bouncer designed to shatter the opponent's confidence and morale.

The story is told of the batsman who sported the latest and most fashionable cricket gear when he faced a hostile reception from the Yorkshireman. Fred clean-bowled him with the first delivery. The batsman passed him on the long trek back to the pavilion and murmured: 'Good ball, Trueman.'

'Aye, and it wasn't worth your while getting dressed up for it, was it?' said Fred.

Yorkshire played an annual friendly match against the pupils at Ampleforth College, and Fred decided to inject a little mischief into the game. The opening batsman, quaking at the thought of facing Fred, was even more disconcerted when Trueman started to pace out his full run. Fred ordered wicket-keeper Jimmy Binks to stand well back. And he glared with menace at the now completely demoralised college player. What the youngster didn't know was that Fred did not have a ball in his hand. Jimmy knew, and so did all the other fielders. Fred came thundering in with mop of black hair bouncing and his feet thudding. He let fly with the non-existent ball, followed through, Jimmy Binks slapped his gloves together as though catching the ball, and the full team leaped and screamed 'Howzat!' The batsman almost disintegrated. He started to walk back to the pavilion and confided to the umpire: 'I never even saw it!'

Fred told me the story of how he acquired his first 'ball'. Do you remember visiting fairs — or feasts, as we called them. Apart from dodgems, the Shamrock, chair o' planes, and other rides, we had rifle ranges, pop-guns, and coconut shies, and it was from this stall Fred pinched the ball destined to play an important role in his bowling development.

He said: 'I painted it red and bowled my coconut ball at a dustbin lid for hours.'

We will never forget his streamlined run-up, cart-wheeling action, and devastating power.

Fred has lasted. He doesn't like being described as 'an ex-cricketer'. He said: 'It makes me feel that I am on the scrap heap.'

That will never happen to the man Harold Wilson termed 'the greatest living Yorkshireman'. And who are we to argue ...

Fred, for one, would not dispute the late prime minister's claim because he had never been prone to undue modesty. When he was asked to suggest a title for his autobiography, he had no hesitation in proposing: 'The definitive volume on the finest bloody fast bowler that ever drew breath.' The publisher declined on the grounds that it was a true claim but rather lengthy and they settled for *Balls of Fire*.

Fred and me have been mates for years, and we go back to the days when the late England and Yorkshire paceman Bill Bowes — a journalist — returned to the *Yorkshire Evening Post* to say: 'I've seen a lad in the nets at Headingley and he will be a bowling revelation. He's got everything. Thank God he was born in Yorkshire.' Fred is fiercely proud of his Yorkshire birthright, and the record books show that he played 459 matches for his beloved county and collected 1,745 wickets. He took 307 in 67 games for England.

Many stories about Fred are of doubtful authenticity and liberally embellished. He wasn't even on tour when it was reported that he had addressed an Indian potentate as 'Gunga Din'. But one tale with a grain of truth is the time he answered a query about the derivation of his nickname. He said: 'People started calling me "Fiery" because it rhymes with Fred just like "Typhoon" rhymes with Tyson.' England requires bowlers of the calibre of Fred Trueman and Frank Tyson if we are to match the current Australians, otherwise the coveted Ashes will have a permanent home Down Under. 'God forbid', said Fred.

Mavis Had a Word for It

We call her 'Our Mavis' even though we are not related. She is a mum and a granny, and has so much love in her tiny frame that everyone who gains her friendship regards her as 'ours'.

She is small. So is her husband, 'Our Dennis'. But they are giants when it comes to lending a helping hand, raising laughter and launching parties. They are both proud of their Yorkshire birthright. When they have a 'bun fight', they dispense with the dainty egg-and-cress sandwiches and have been known to fill a groaning table with black puddings, tripe, cow-heel, ham, and fat and bread. They enjoy a sing-song. They have joy in their outsize hearts. And Our Mavis and Our Dennis will never be short of family and friends.

We have shared gales of laughter which usually emanate from the sayings of Our Mavis. She has taken 'saying the wrong thing' to the standard of an art form. And she vies with my pal Chick for gems of unconscious humour.

Chick was an old-time boxer who became a very successful businessman. He had me in stitches when he talked about his lads and said: 'My kids don't know they are born. They live in a fool's parrot house.'

I thought that would never be capped. But Our Mavis has produced a few belters in her time, and she believes that her work should be published in what she once termed 'The Alec Book of Guinness'.

Our Mavis sat in front of the television, and the announcer told viewers to get a pen and paper to take down an address. She jumped to her feet, ran to the drawer and asked the TV presenter to 'Hang on a minute. Don't read it out yet. Wait until I get my pen.' He seemed to listen to Our Mavis, too. Just as we all do.

Television appears to fascinate the lady. She usually feels involved in the action when she watches a thriller, and she did not entirely fall for the wiles and guiles of one particular screen villain. Mavis wilted at one of his dirty tricks and commented: 'Let him swim in his own stew.' Then there was another 'baddy' who earned the disapproval of the much-loved mum and she told the assembled family: 'Don't worry about him. He'll get his upandcommance.'

You can see that Our Mavis is a bit of a genius. And she provided further evidence of this claim when her spouse complained of a hangover. Dennis's ministering angel advised: 'You want the hare that bit the dog.' Of course he knew exactly what she meant and he nipped smartly down to the local for the cure.

There was an occasion when the children were a bit fractious. And Mavis had to take action to quieten the brood. She thought for a moment and came up with the answer. She mustered a glare of annoyance and warned the kiddies: 'If you don't behave, I'll run away and join the British Legion.' That daunting threat was enough to silence her offspring for good.

Our Mavis once lost her voice. It must have been a result of one of the many sing-along sessions which invariably saw Our Dennis performing the aria 'Baby has slipped down the plug-hole'. Once again the children were a little too noisy and playful. And Our Mavis's hoarse whispers had little effect on the capers. She coughed and managed to splutter: 'If I could shout, I'd clout you.' But that muted threat was not true. Our Mavis would never look back in anger and she is not quite big enough to throw her weight about.

My mother-in-law once told me she did not like being at the seaside because of the seagulls 'hoovering about'. And she would make a good mate for Our Mavis, who was a bit upset one day and started to worry about a couple of her babes. She produced the purler: 'I can't help ferreting about them.'

When she had a bit of trouble walking, her thoughts turned to a walking stick to aid her, because she was adamant that the doctor wouldn't get her 'on one of those zithers'. She meant zimmers, of course, but we didn't have the heart to tell her.

Every family has a 'Mavis'. She could be a mother, granny, auntie, sister or cousin. They are ladies who handle a crisis with calm acceptance. The totally unexpected fails to ruffle their self control. The girls — young and elderly — portray genuine sympathy. They roll up their sleeves and tackle the most mundane and demanding chores with cheerful enthusiasm. They breeze through life with a ready solution to any problem, and who cares if they mix up words and so often produce illogical solutions to everyday difficulties?

My mother Norah was 'Our Mavis'. She told me: 'I'm not wearing my new teeth until I get used to them.' She swore that her acute deafness had improved since she was equipped with the hearing aid she left in its original wrapping in the sideboard drawer. We smiled with kindly indulgence on Norah's verbal gaffs. Just as Our Dennis did when Our Mavis made an unforgettable statement.

It is quite a time since we had one of Our Mavis's famous Yorkshire parties. No doubt when she reads this she will decide that another is called for, and I will not hesitate to accept her invitation, if only to listen for one or more of her verbal hiccups.

You can see why we call her 'Our Mavis'.

Veritable Feast on a Platter

It was at Barkers music store in Leeds where teenagers — and golden oldies — shopped for records to boost their respective collections of cherished 78s.

We played them on a radiogram which had a wireless and turntable inside a walnut cabinet. It was quite a handsome piece of furniture bought in a sale from Vallance and Davisons opposite the Corn Exchange. Our household's pride and joy came with a tin of tiny needles which were regularly changed to protect the records, and our prestigious radiogram also arrived with a complimentary velvet-covered duster for wiping clean the Decca, His Master's Voice, Parlophone and other popular recordings.

It was years later before we called the 'platters' by the modern name of 'discs', and my purchase from Barkers was a jazz record of Joe Daniels and his Hot Shots. It has the word 'Drumnastics' on the label surrounding the hole in the centre of the record, and this was a clue to Joe's contribution — a break in the music for a drum solo from the South African-born musician.

I bought records from Kitchens as well as Barkers, and also patronised Stringers bookstall in Leeds market where you could buy second-hand novels and records and part exchange them for another.

But Barkers was a magnet for youngsters like me, and I believe it was the first music store in the city to provide kiosks with earphones for private listening. I spent many a happy half-hour in my lunch break listening to records in one of Barkers' booths, and invariably returned to my afternoon duties without buying one. In fact it was only because an assistant demanded 'Are you ever going to honour us with a sale?' that I felt honour-bound to produce a shilling or two for Joe Daniels and his Hot Shots.

The folk at home objected to my choice of music. My parents and visiting relatives much preferred songs by John McCormick, Vera Lynn, the Companion de le Chanson, Ann Shelton, Bing Crosby and Frederick Ferrari to the musical outpourings of my Dixieland jazz idols.

Joe's record was the first of many, and my hoard grew to decent proportions and was loaned to a youth project at St

Augustine's Church, Harehills, Leeds, never to be seen by yours truly again. That was more than fifty years ago, and if the present occupiers of St Augustine's should come across a dusty pile of 'discs' in the crypt, I will cheerfully collect them. But I am only kidding. My records, without the vital radiogram, turntable, needles and velvet duster, would be a useless acquisition in these days of sophisticated and computerised methods of music making.

Joe Daniels was born over ninety years ago and he formed a band to play in England immediately after the war. He was also a member of Harry Roy's Ragamuffins and he was still active on the jazz scene in the early part of the 1990s.

It's a little known fact that Joe was the younger brother of the magician Sirdani, who toured the Moss Empire circuit with his illusions, tricks and a catch-phrase which gained national recognition. Sirdani was known as the man who regularly told volunteer stooges picked from the audience: 'Don't be fright'. And this fine example of verbal nonsense tickled the English sense of humour and was used in general conversation for years.

Sirdani was magical in more ways than one, and so was the traditional jazz era in Yorkshire which enjoyed a boom in popularity — particularly in Leeds, Bradford and Wakefield — before the dawn of rock and roll and the domination of guitar-twanging groups.

Where There's a Will

It was a chap called Dick Needham who listed the seven ages of man and summed them up as: spills, drills, thrills, hills, ills, pills and wills. And it is that final macabre subject we have on the agenda for discussion, dear reader. The Last Will and Testament.

It all started when the Lovely Maureen embarked on her current bout of spring cleaning. And her annual dumping of all things dear to me but described by her as junk and rubbish. Her rummaging went as far as the tin chocolate box — you must have one — where we keep our marriage licence, my RAF paybook in case I am called up again, the dog licence for Sandy who died twenty-eight years ago, paying-in books for the first furniture we bought on the never-never in 1952, and other important documents like a guide to home-brewing and my wartime identity card with the number KGHU 55/3.

The Lovely Maureen's fingers flicked through the contents with the dexterity of a bank teller counting fivers. She tossed one or two precious items away — to be secretly replaced by yours truly at a later date — when, without warning, she released a blood-curdling yell of 'Oh no!' The Lovely Maureen had discovered that I had not acceded to the vehement request she made in 1970 that I should make a will.

It was in that year I had regular pains in the region of my ticker. It turned out to be nothing more serious than indigestion, but before that diagnosis my ministering angel pointed out that, if I was contemplating leaving this mortal coil, it was only right that I should leave my affairs in apple-pie order.

'Obviously we will be sorry to see you go and hope that you can stay a little longer', she said with a comforting wink. 'But if there is any danger of you departing, don't you think you ought to make your will? All that business with probate and so forth can cause complications', she added, 'and I would rather get on with my mourning and the wearing of my widow's weeds than the inconvenience of dressing up for a trip to the solicitor's office to swear a few oaths.'

She was right of course. It was damned inconsiderate of me to think about dying before making the right sort of provision. And I crossed myself and swore on the Holy Bible that I would drop everything and make an appointment to draw up my Last Will and Testament in the presence of our family lawyer Mr Ronald Teeman.

In fact I got as far as the door of Teeman, Teeman, Teeman and Teeman, as Ronald's one-man firm was known in those far-off days. But I did not enter. I reasoned that, instead of lining Ronald's pocket with a guinea or probably two, I would adopt a DIY approach to the problem. I went to our local post office and bought a will form. It all sounded very simple. But I never completed the incidentals because a warning in small print told me that it was safer to have a solicitor draw up the will because DIY wills had — like bad cheques — a habit of bouncing.

So I changed my mind about dying. I simply stuck the blank form in an equally blank envelope and placed it in the tin box. It rested there until the prying Lovely Maureen discovered my grievous omission. Quite honestly, my life has not been worth living since then.

Yorkshireman have an old saying: 'Where there's a will — there's a relative.' And I recall an occasion when Mr Thompson, a chap in his seventies, was preparing to meet his maker. Mr Thompson had his local doctor and priest at his bedside. And the comforting cleric was a necessity because the poorly pensioner had led a miserly — nay greedy and grasping — miserable existence from the day he could pinch a penny. It was once said of Mr Thompson that he only breathed in. He was mean to the extreme. Mr Thompson ignored the Yorkshire adage 'He who takes and never gives may last for years but never lives.'

The doctor held his hand and reflected: 'Well, Mr Thompson, you have had your three score years and ten you know.'

Mr Thompson raised his head from the pillow and wheezed: 'Nay doctor. You haven't allowed for VAT.'

He was that type of man. But he made a will, and his fortune went to free-spending heirs who erected a tombstone with an appropriate inscription. It read: 'Here lies Mr Thompson, a financial genius, who added, multiplied and never subtracted. His grateful relatives divided.'

I looked at my blank will form today and vowed: 'I will definitely make a will. Honestly I will.' But hang on a

moment. Didn't I make and sign a will when I was doing my National Service? I feel sure that I did. I distinctly remember appending my signature to some sort of legal document before embarking on the good ship *The Empress of Australia* and sailing to Egypt to serve my king and country. I recall that I left everything to my mother, Norah Morgan. I left her gratuities, accrued from my twenty-eight shillings a week wage, my stamp collection, a Leeds United autographed programme with the names of Jim Twomey, Aubrey Powell, David Cochrane and Tom Holley scribbled inside, and a framed certificate to prove that I had made my first Holy Communion. I added to those prized possessions the phrase 'and all my worldly wealth, goods and chattels'. No doubt it is still gathering dust in the RAF Records Office at Gloucester.

There is only one thing I can do. I must make an appointment with Mr Ronald Teeman. I have sampled Dick Needham's spills drills, thrills, hills, ills and pills. It's time to draw up the will — not that it will be read for another score years, or so. I am sure of that.

Brushing Shoulders with Royalty

It has been my happy lot to mix with royalty on occasion, which is invariably an exciting and challenging experience for journalists searching for a tale and hanging on every word emanating from such distinguished persons. You wait with increasing anticipation for a quote or gesture which will keep scoop-hungry editors happy. And the royals usually oblige — often unintentionally — to provide the right sort of copy and smiling pictures.

My first encounter with the world of members of our royal family occurred a few years ago when a radiant Princess Margaret arrived at St James's Hospital, Leeds, to open a new building. Twisted red ropes with brass ends stuck in bollards were in place to mark the route Princess Margaret would follow. And also, I suspect, to keep her away from a ward of geriatrics who were not expecting a visit. We dogged her footsteps and those of her entourage as she toured the bright and shiny corridors. And it looked as though it would be a routine story, with nothing more to add than she was greatly impressed with the improved facilities. But — without any warning — Princess Margaret unclasped one of the ropes and made it a memorable day for many aged and wandering invalids. She brought a ray of sunshine into their humdrum existence and gave the retinue of reporters the story it wanted.

But newshounds were not present at Leeds Civic Hall the day a certain member of the House of Windsor — now deceased, I hasten to add — threw a monumental bout of tantrums, with tears and stamping of feet, because she could not take home to London a glittering chandelier she admired so much. It was the late John Rafferty — one of the most popular lord mayors ever to hold the ancient and dignified office — who told me the tale. But we have only scanty details about the unsightly hullabaloo. And a civic veil was drawn over the unseemly outburst.

John lost a leg in an accident as a child, and he never tired of recalling an incident which happened many years after the amputation. He was involved in a car crash near St James's Hospital. Police and firemen were called to the scene, and the

rescuers started to pull the occupants from the crushed vehicles. 'Get a stretcher. There's a chap here with a leg off!' hollered one of the ambulancemen, and John recovered consciousness just in time to hear a cry of sheer panic.

John often recalled the visit made to Leeds by Princess Elizabeth, when the lord mayor was obviously a mite awe-stricken, and probably a little overcome by the solemnity and enormity of the occasion. In those days, members of the royal household were not as accessible as they are today. The red carpet was stretched out. The princess arrived and our number one citizen walked with a degree of trepidation to greet her. He stuck out his hand, searched frantically for the right words, and blurted out: 'How's your father?' The queen-to-be murmured: 'Do you mean His Majesty the King?'

Prince Philip's attitude to the press is not always friendly, and I remember hanging on to his coat tails, and verbal pearls, at one function where he repeated his oft-quoted opinion of a national newspaper he regarded as 'a bloody rag'.

There was another time when we were unable to get close to him at a Scarborough conference as deadlines for the filing of stories came nearer and nearer. But one inspired journalist, of *Daily Herald* fame, made sure that he would have an audience with the outspoken duke. The reporter confided: 'There is one place Philip will have to go and that is the little boys' room. I know where it is and I will be there waiting for him.' He waited almost two hours and the guest of honour eventually arrived. The intrepid correspondent slid to the esteemed gentleman's side. He introduced himself and asked a pertinent question, to which the eminent gentleman replied: 'This is hardly the place or the time for such a conversation. Good afternoon.'

But there was an occasion at Epsom racecourse when the noble prince was given the mother and father of a ticking off by an irate reporter. Prince Philip walked through the pressroom. He picked up a ringing telephone and barked: 'He's not in.' The correspondent, waiting for a fixed-time call from his office, was, like Queen Victoria, 'not amused' — and he let the intruder know with a tirade of earthy Fleet Street lingo.

Princess Anne scowled at me, and another reprobate reporter, at Pontefract, but our hearts melted when we saw her break away from an official group to exchange pleasantries with a few excited parents and their equally elated offspring.

But the queen will always be number one in the affections of many. I remember with glee the day she attended tricentenary celebrations at Selby Abbey, and how the packed congregation waited for her arrival and stood for half an hour or so in the pews waiting for the sovereign to appear. The late Jack Hickes, a freelance news photographer and once the scourge of rival cameramen when he was in opposition at the *Yorkshire Evening News,* stationed himself in the abbey and looked in vain for his reporter colleague Neil. He eventually put in an appearance and his gaze wandered in search of Jack.

'Neil, Neil', hissed Jack, 'Neil ...'

Hundreds of worshippers immediately dropped to their knees.

The queen turned up ten minutes later with the congregation still on its 'benders', and I am sure she would have enjoyed a little giggle had anyone acquainted her of Jack's command.

As I said at the beginning, it has been my happy lot to mix with royalty ... long may it reign!

The Hard Men of Soccer

There was a sporting crisis in our family at the weekend when young James's shin pads went missing. It was a case of panic stations. We launched a full-scale search of my daughter's happy homestead but failed to unearth the missing items. It looked as though one of the stars of Guiseley Dynamo's all-conquering team would have to withdraw from the action or play without equipment that is deemed so vital to the protection of little limbs.

But is it? When we were kids, we scorned such pampered padding. We rolled our socks down to the ankles in the style of Roy of the Rovers and the Cannonball Kid, and, if we felt we required insulation from a wild-kicking opponent, we stuffed rolled-up comics or magazines down our stockings. But this scant regard for the safety of legs with sparrows' kneecaps did not imply any immunity to pain. It was simply a case of not being able to afford luxuries like proper shin-guards.

Many parents had all on to buy second-hand football boots. I mean those with the bulbous toecaps and half-inch-long leather studs sticking from the soles. If either part of the boot connected with a rival's torso, you made a mark designed to decorate the unlucky recipient for life.

Balls were as heavy as treacle puddings. Laces guaranteed to lacerate temples were also a hazard. It took an intrepid lunatic to jump from a bottomless morass and head the soggy sphere when it was booted sky-high. You could always pick out a regular header. He stood out in a crowd if only because he lacked a neck. His head was buried between his shoulder blades and his chin was thrust on his chest. He usually looked like Neanderthal Man and he spoke with the clarity and coherence of a grunting gorilla.

They were hard men. They were not vicious. They were tough and uncompromising, and when it came to washing off the after-match mud they were the first to duck under a cold-water tap when lesser folk contemplated and often declined the freezing horrors of those primitive ablutions.

I was determined to become a footballer of repute. My ambitions were fired by the performances of such schoolboy

stars as Billy Knott and Billy Roberts, who were cast in the
same mould as the other East Leeds legends Daddy Melia and
Laurie Dooker. They drew colossal crowds to local games
before the days when Paul Reaney, Paul Madeley and Kevin
Hector starred for Leeds City Boys.

But I was useless. I looked the part in my green and white
strip with boots inherited from a lad called Donald Butterfield.
My trouble was I had two left legs, a heart as big as a raisin,
and a total lack of relish for bodily contact. I reached
international standard at keeping out of the action. My plan
was simple. If the ball went one way, I went the other. But I
almost had my moment of soccer glory.

I was sixteen years years old and *Evening Post* sports
editor John Bapty sent me with a photographer to Elland
Road for a pre-season picture. In those 1940 days, players did
a couple of hours training — probably three times a week —
then sprinted for a bus to take them to Charlie Mahon's
Billiard and Snooker Saloon in the city centre. When we
arrived, the dash to town had already taken place and players
at the stadium were a bit thin on the ground. There were
Ginger Coyne, Gerald Henry, Jim McGraw, Jim Twomey and
David Cochrane, and I joined them in a posed picture for our
cameraman. The photograph duly appeared and my presence
was explained in the caption which read something like: 'It

was the thrill of a lifetime for teenager John Morgan when he trained with his football heroes. John will probably join Leeds United's nursery team the Stormcocks.'

The following day I was approached by scouts from several clubs. But the most persistent chap was from Bradford Park Avenue who offered me all sorts of attractive fringe benefits to have a trial with his club. He then offered to dispense with the trial if I would sign on the dotted line. It took weeks before I convinced him hat I was not a budding Stanley Matthews or a potential Tom Finney.

Park Avenue was always my first choice when Leeds United were away, and we rejoiced in the magic of soccer's clown prince, Len Shackleton, the true-blue amateur Jackie Gibbons and the agility of goalkeeper Chick Farr, whose drastic short-back-and-sides suggested he had his hair cut at Kirkstall Forge or that he had just had a near-miss with a guillotine.

Jim Milburn of everlasting Leeds United fame was one of my favourite hard men. He used to stick his chest in front of full-blooded drives without flinching. We had a centre forward paid to score goals, but whenever a penalty kick was granted, full-back Jim was whistled up to crash the ball, and sometimes the keeper, into the net. The reporting vernacular in those days was descriptive to say the least. And we read with joy that Jim's shots 'rattled the rigging' or 'threatened to burst the onion bag'.

Jim worked at Tetley's Brewery, and years after his playing career ended I told him of an incident which occurred when Leeds United played Manchester City. The visiting team had a spokesman in flamboyant Rodney Marsh, who was detailed to approach the Leeds management with the complaint that there were no suitable electric points in the changing room for the players to plug in their hair driers. At first Jim scoffed at the tale. But he fell about when he discovered that the story was authentic. 'What a load of cissies', said my hero.

But they are not. The game is still for real men — even those who sport earrings and other sparkling medallions. It inflames passion and produces more anguish, thrills, heart-breaking failure and glorious triumphs than any other ball game. Only soccer could draw from such a dignitary as Cardinal Basil Hume the request: 'Please play the theme from *Match of the Day* at my funeral.'

Getting Around to It

On my birthday I received a present of 'a round tuit'. It is small, flat, obviously cylindrical and inscribed with words of encouragement, exhortation and explanation. But before I let you into the secret, may I unburden my soul and tell you — with shame bordering on remorse — that I am the world's worst when it comes to do-it-yourself.

I am to DIY what Audley Harrison is to the Ballet Rambert or Herod to baby-sitting. My initial attempt at the creation of something useful and inexpensive was fired by a neighbour's double-quick erection of a garden shed with sliding doors, windows and patio. I opted for something a little less ambitious — a three-legged stool. It was a disaster and almost a killer. The woodwork came in a pack with legs already shaped and smoothed. All I had to do was glue them on to a cross piece, insert them in holes in the sandpapered seat, and paint the finished article. What could be more simple? I paraded my handiwork for the lovely but querulous Maureen, then eight months into potential motherhood.

'Is it safe?' she asked.

'As houses', was my confident reply. 'Stand on it, if you don't believe me.'

My ever-trusting spouse — a sort of stool pigeon — perched on my green-coloured example of British craftsmanship. And it will always be a mystery why she did not precipitate the forthcoming offspring into the world there and then. The legs shot to three points of the compass like Exocet missiles. There was a yell of pain as one flying bolt seared my ankle and an even more piercing shriek of animal agony as another scored a direct hit on Tim, next door's tomcat. The other leg vanished, never to be seen again.

My next bout of DIY fever was inspired when I was given an exorbitant quote of £27 for the digging out, hard coring and laying down of cement for a drive and garage base.

'If I can't do it for half that price, I'll eat the concrete', I promised the wavering wife.

Unfortunately, my excavations were so deep I kept the concrete mixing firm on overtime throughout the weekend. They made ten deliveries. I was up to my blue-circled eyes in

Trumix, and the hard fact was I had spent six times more than the professionals' 'outrageous' estimate. The base at that address is so thick you could drive a division of Sherman tanks over it and not dent the surface. But the main fault was the base slopes. Being a complete novice, I never thought to install a drain and every time it rained with any intensity the garage flooded. My explanation to the lovely Maureen that it doubled as home for the car and an indoor swimming pool for the family didn't hold water, if you will pardon the pun.

Decorating came next. We really went to town with our money and paid up to half a crown a roll for brown-flowered wallpaper for the master bedroom in our one-up and one-down. You must have seen the circus clowns in their slapstick paste and paper routine. They do it for laughs. I did it for real. I climbed the ladder with the sticky, soggy paper draped in front of my size nines, which went through brown flowers with every trembling step. Eventually I was left with a ragged piece about six inches deep. The rest of the strip drooped on my curls or stuck with limpet-like adhesion to my boots.

I should have taken a leaf (a brown one?) out of my Irish neighbour's book. Pat tacked his paper on the walls and used thousands of tiny nails to hold it in place. When his front door opened and a draught got behind the decorations, they rippled. And it was quite effective when the wallpaper sported a nautical design. You gained the distinct impression that you were on an ocean-going cruise.

My venture into the electrical world was quite a shocker. I completed one wiring job but failed to ascertain whether or not the power was going through.

'Stick your finger in the socket', I laughingly suggested to the lady in my life.

And before I could stop her, she did. A few thousand volts certainly make the hair curl, and I've since learned that such a shock is good for a bad back. I can vouch for that claim. The Lovely Maureen has had a bad back every since.

Gardening came next. I had a gentleman helper who pleaded with me not to meddle with the plot after I had hoed up a couple of his rows of spring onions in the honest belief that they were weeds. I even thought radishes grew in bunches and thought my crop had failed when they came up singly. I once mixed too strong a brew of liquid manure, and it burned the roots of my rose trees and killed off a long row of once-healthy bushes. The operation drew from my long-suffering spouse the remark: 'When it comes to horticulture — my husband is totally non compost mentis. He is a divi!'

So you can see, dear reader, that I am a man who needs to be looked after. I require a guardian angel. I'm not safe to be let loose with hammer, paint brush, screwdriver or spade. But, because of my ineptitude, the list of jobs to be done has 'growed and growed'. And that is why I received that special present.

When the Lovely Maureen suggests that I oil the hinges on the door, paint the outhouse or replace the cracked window, I always promise: 'I'll do it when I get around to it.' And so 'a round tuit' arrived. It is a tiny disc bearing the message: 'This is the round tuit you have always wanted. Now you have one get on with the work.' All I can say is, give me the tools and I'll make a real botch of the jobs.

The Job of a Lifetime

Nearly sixty years have elapsed since a curly-haired, wide-eyed and totally naive little lad cut himself free from his doting mother's apron strings. He headed for the big world outside the maternal cosseting and he embarked on a career in journalism, albeit as a messenger boy, with the Yorkshire Conservative Newspaper Company Limited. He was ordered to report to the offices of the *Yorkshire Evening Post,* Albion Street, Leeds, at nine o'clock sharp. And he arrived at 7.30 am simply because he was scared of being late and also because he had not slept a wink the night before he was to become gainfully employed.

I will never forget that morning. The tram from the terminus at the foot of Gipton Approach, Leeds 9, had a sprinkling of passengers — and a conductress who looked for all the world like the 1940s screen lovely Veronica Lake. The 'clippie' adopted the same distinctive hairstyle, with the 'bang', as it was called, sweeping down one side of her pretty face and almost covering one eye. I remember offering a coin and asking with grown-up pride for 'A workman's return, please'.

That trip to the city centre was one of mixed feelings. It was tinged with red-faced excitement, eager anticipation, mortal dread and the occasional threat of tears. I strolled to my working destiny with as much confidence as my quaking heart could muster. But I fought shy of entering the famous *Yorkshire Evening Post* archway — with hanging gas lamp — until the starting time dictated by Mr Taylor. He was the kindly man who gave me the job and offered the princely sum of ten shillings (fifty pence) for a five-and-a-half day week.

But Mr Taylor also had a welcome surprise for me. The firm decided that day to add a twenty-five per cent war bonus to all earnings, and this took my wages to twelve shillings and sixpence minus twopence stoppages. My joy was unconfined.

The rest of that day is a blur, although I do remember inadvertently setting off a fire extinguisher, and I will also recall to my dying day the embarrassment of my first visit to the canteen. It was lunchtime, and ninety-nine per cent of the diners tucked into bangers and mash followed by spotted dick and custard. But not me. I unwrapped a parcel of my mother's 'banjoes'. She believed in the maxim 'strength goes in at the mouth'. She never subscribed to dainty egg-and-cress sandwiches, cut into tiny triangles, with the crusts trimmed off. She preferred to feed her offspring with king-sized portions, and her sarnies were of the wedge type with thick slices wrapped round equally generous fillings.

But on that first day she surpassed herself. She made sure that I was in no danger of starving. She packed enough food to feed the Biblical five thousand. I pulled one sandwich from the wrapping and waded in with mouth stretched like the entrance to Stump Cross Cavern. And I was suddenly aware of a stunned silence. Flashing knives and forks were stilled. Diners paused to look with horror, or admiration, at the new kid stuffing what appeared to be a full loaf and a pound or two of polony down his throat. I felt the gaze of a hundred eyes. I stopped in mid-bite. I gathered my grub in an untidy bundle, clasped it to my chest, and fled. The following day I clutched sixpence in my sticky hand and ordered bangers and mash, and spotted dick and custard, and it was my daily lunchtime order for years to come.

I remember the thrill of my first published item — a story thirty paragraphs long, reduced by the sub-editor's thick black pencil to a nine-word line. I was upset but not destroyed. I was determined to have scoops and modestly admit that my dreams of exclusive stories eventually materialised.

But today I reflect on the stories that got away. I remember interviewing the oldest inhabitant of a Yorkshire village. He was 103 not out and he attributed his longevity to 'a good life, moderation in all things and a pint of spring water every day'. The elixir gurgled from a cliff face and the veteran used to walk to the spot to drink the crystal-clear but evil-tasting liquid. I wrote the story on a Wednesday, and the tale was due to appear the following Monday, which was the day after the veteran was to have celebrated birthday number 104. The saga never appeared. It was suggested that I contacted the old fellow on the eve of publication, and I did, only to find that he had breathed his last when walking up the hill to fill his glass with the life-giving beverage. The magic properties had obviously disappeared — and so did my story.

Another tale which went begging was the one of a chap who 'rode shotgun' on a Sammy Ledgard bus. He was a conductor. He was getting on in years, and he became more than a little agitated when threatened by a hulking male passenger. The route took the bus along lonely roads and in and out of hamlets in the Yorkshire Dales. And so he bought himself a rifle and ammunition for protection. I was assigned to the story, and obviously checked the facts with the conductor's immediate boss who knew nothing about the fellow carrying arms. The governor was distraught. He investigated our claim and then admitted:

'It's true. He does have a gun on board the bus. But if you print the story we will have to sack him. He has a wife and dependants. He is due to retire within a couple of years, and if he is dismissed, he will lose his pension.'

What did we do? Did we adopt the motto 'Publish and be damned'? Of course not. We killed the story. The chap surrendered his gun. He was given an office job, and he and his wife and dependants all lived happily ever after. And so have I.

King of the Tipsters

It was one writer or another who penned the observation: 'When the country is in recession, we are asked to give up the things our grandparents never knew.'

There is a lot of truth in the claim when you consider the miraculous advances in the last hundred years. Some of the things we take for granted were not even envisaged by our forebears. They would probably have scoffed with sheer disbelief — like we did — if someone had suggested that man would walk on the moon or Leeds United would win the FA Cup.

But many of my late relatives — father, uncles and cousins — enjoyed something denied to me and many followers of the Sport of Kings. They worked on a *Yorkshire Post* publication called the *Mid-Day Sporting Special* which carried articles and tips by Ranger, the Duke, Julius, White Knight and many others. It was a popular newspaper but ended with the outbreak of war, and my dad, who was a successful sixpence-each-way backer, must have had withdrawal symptoms when the *Mid-Day Sporting Special* drifted into oblivion.

I felt the same when the *Sporting Pink* died a premature death with the closure of the *Yorkshire Evening News* in December 1963, and I still miss the unforgettable *Sporting Life* which sadly closed a few years ago. In one idle moment I calculated that I had read, from cover to cover, at least 15,000 copies of the *Sporting Life* during my working years, and my wife, the Lovely Maureen, suggested: 'It is a pity you had nothing better to do.'

My thoughts regularly turn to the the *Mid-Day Sporting Special* and the *Sporting Pink*. The 'Pink' was affectionately known by locals as the 'Tisher', and many were armed with this 'racing bible' as they caught special coaches run by Wallace Arnold, Heaps Tours and others to the various sporting venues in the county.

Pontefract was always a magnet for punters from the West Riding, and we often travelled the few miles by train, with the 'Pink' folded under our arms as we walked the last few hundred yards to the enclosures. Decades ago the walkway

was dotted with stalls where you could buy a mug of tea, sandwiches generously filled with pork and stuffing, and pie and peas smothered in gravy and mint sauce. You could also dip into your pocket money for butterscotch, crumbly cinder toffee, liquorice bootlaces, sweet mushrooms covered in coconut, Highland toffee, chocolate-covered monkey nuts, and the inevitable Pontefract Cakes.

Apart from the different forms of sustenance on sale at 'Ponty', you could spend a few coppers on buying 'racing certainties' from colourful tipsters. One of the most persuasive members of the tipping ranks was a Leeds chap called Ruston. He not only advertised a postal service in the *Mid-Day Sporting Special* and the *Sporting Pink* but also entertained listeners with his spiel outside the entrance to the Pontefract grandstand. Ruston usually impressed punters by throwing down a wad of notes on the grass beneath his feet. He would say: 'There is £100 in that bundle and I will give it to any man who disputes the fact that I tipped Hairylegs to win at Nottingham at twenty to one last week.' Ruston was never challenged to hand over the cash, but there was one night in the Green Man in Pontefract when the cash disappeared from his pocket. When the thief unwrapped the top £1 note from the wad, he discovered layers of toilet paper. The 'hundred pounds' was £99 short.

There was another man who traded under the name of Tiny the Turf Adviser who dressed in tweed jacket, with horseshoe pin stuck in his cravat, jodhpurs, riding boots and bowler. But Ruston was the king of the local tippers, and he was often accompanied by a young chap clad in jockey silks with the regulation breeches, cap and whip. Ruston pointed at the lad and hollered:

'See this jockey here. He can ride anything. We have to strap him down when we put him on a bus. He rode for Captain Boyd-Rochfort but he was sacked because he knew too much. He lost his job because he backed winners. And he is here today to give you the benefit of his knowledge.'

The jockey certainly looked the part but he did not utter a single word. He left it to Ruston to drum up the business.

Those were the days when the late Tommy Melia worked on the courses. He hailed from a family connected with the selling of newspapers for many years. Tommy worked for the *Yorkshire Evening Post* and his job was to operate the Stop Press printing machine in the Bush van which visited every sporting location. It was his justifiable boast that within four minutes of Yorkshire bowlers taking a wicket at Headingley he could have it in the Stop Press and on sale in the best ring at Pontefract or any other course. Tommy was brilliant — like so many men who loved and lived for the 'Tisher', and *The Post* and *News*.

A Brush with Destiny

Sam is a groundsman. He is gnarled but sturdy as an oak tree. He is tanned from days in the sun, and he tends his cricket field with the loving devotion young bucks feel for the feminine object of their syrupy adulation. Sam's wife Sara often claims with justification: 'He's married to that field. He thinks more about it that he does of me.'

And Sam adds credence to her opinion when he talks about the vast acreage as though it was a woman. Sam sucks on his pipe and murmurs 'She's showing her age' or 'She's looking better now that she's had a drop of sun on her back'. And passers-by often think that the poor old fellow has been touched with the 'doolally stick'. Sam couldn't give a threepenny curse for the opinions of others. It takes a lot to upset this inflappable son of the soil. But he almost had a dicky fit the other day when he said: 'Summat untoward happened, like.'

Sam had put in a few hours' solid work on the pitch. It was like a billiard board. It was fresh and green. There wasn't a blade of grass out of place. There wasn't an offending weed in sight. He had swept the wicket, and it was as neat, tidy and trim as Sara's front room which was dusted every day and used only occasionally for Sunday tea. Sam was at peace with the world. He produced his Thermos flask from a bag, unwrapped his sandwiches, and settled in the old chair he kept in the shed which also housed his lawn-mower and weedkiller. Sam ate his lunch, closed his eyes for forty winks, and woke up an hour later, refreshed in mind, body and spirit.

He stretched his arms, walked out of his hide-away — and he came to a full stop. He could not believe the scene before his eyes. The crease was covered with muck, scraps of paper and what appeared to be flower petals. Sam was — as he said — 'Proper upset, like, and scandalised, like. It was like a tip, like.' He dashed back into the shed. He picked up the witch's broom he uses for brushing the sacred turf and he charged to the scene of destruction to brush like a demented charwoman. He piled the dirt, bits and pieces on to a shovel, carried it to the edge of the field and threw the offending muck into a beck bordering the cricket arena. Sam stood and watched the lot — petals and all — drifting on the tiny stream and into the channel leading to the village sewer.

'That's got rid of that', said Sam, and he breathed a sigh of satisfaction when he saw that once again his beloved plot was in apple-pie order.

Sam went home for his tea and — at the stroke of 7pm — he knocked out his pipe and told Sara that he would nip down to the club to have a pint and a game of dominoes, and that he would not be late. He paid for his beer and joined his mate Reg at the domino table. Reg shuffled the dominoes and in walked the local vicar. He is a very gentle man. He is — as Sam says — 'Nice like. But he tends to twitter instead of asserting himself.' The kindly cleric approached Sam rather shyly, clasped his hands as though in prayer and murmured:

'That was a nice little ceremony down at the pitch today. It was Jack Holdgate's last wish that his ashes should be scattered near the crease and I was ever so pleased to comply with his final request.'

Sam's face was a picture. His pipe almost fell from his open mouth. 'By 'eck', he exclaimed. 'Nobody told me about that job. I've weshed Jack down t' river!'

Last requests can often cause a problem or two. And I will always remember the occasion when my aunt died in America where she had lived for many years. She was Castleford-born, and her son and daughter thought it would be appropriate for her head to rest on Yorkshire soil. We were asked to send a tiny packet of Castleford dust to America, and it was duly collected, despatched and placed in the casket. I wrote about the request, and the tale was spotted by a civil servant who sent me a letter expressing concern about people exporting bits of Britain to foreign parts. He wrote tongue-in-cheek:

'If everybody started sending our muck abroad we would have nowt left. Please desist from this practice. Don't do it again.'

I didn't and I was able to tell Sam the tale. He has almost recovered his composure, and the family Jack left behind are oblivious to the fate of their deceased relative.

'Life has to go on, like', says Sam, 'and really Jack could hardly complain about being swept from the crease, like,

because he was never in long enough to make a good innings. It was usually a case of first ball and he was out, like — not that he deserved to be sent up the creek without a paddle.'

Sam was busy at the weekend looking after his pitch. Summer is drawing to a close. The season is almost over, and before long he will be putting on the covers for the winter recess and protecting the strip which is part of his life.

He once delivered a lecture on the preparation of wickets. He stood up before an expectant audience and announced with an authorative timbre in his voice: 'The best thing for wickets is hoss muck.' And he sat down. The chairman obviously expected a longer discourse from Sam. He nudged the speaker in the ribs and murmured: 'Surely there is something more?' Sam stood up again and hollered: 'No — just hoss muck'.

I'll miss him when he goes. I wonder if he has any last requests?

Nappy Days

'Phew!' was my reaction when I picked up a one-year-old laddie the other day. He knew what he had done and, judging by the self-satisfied twinkle in his little blue eyes, he knew that I knew. But could I change his nappy? No sir!

Time was when I thought nothing about transforming an infant from a smelly outcast into a clean and cuddly bundle. The babe would be bathed and beautiful. The mite would be powdered, perfumed and welcomed on any lap.

But things are not the same now. We had nappies until the Americans came along with diapers and disposables. Nappies were often home-made. But many a domestic budget stretched to the purchase of fluffy towelling squares which were folded into a triangle to cover the baby's nether regions. The points met in the centre and we inserted a safety pin to hold the nappy in place. Then we would encase the lot in a pair of plastic pants which were definitely an improvement on those old rubber garments which rubbed red weals round chubby children's legs.

The problem of kiddies' toilet issues can be a constant source of worry and, at times, humour.

'What are bowels?' asked a teacher.

'A E I O U', replied one diminutive pupil.

'Where are the bowels?' persisted the frustrated mistress.

'I don't know — my mother keeps moving them', said another child.

Then we had a letter from the mum of a boy whose constipation kept him at home from school. The missive read: 'Johnny can't come because he can't go. I have given him something to make him go. And when he has been he can come.'

I remember another lady writing: 'My boy is suffering from dire rear. Please oblige Mrs Thompson.' It was amazing how many mothers finished notes to teachers with the request 'please oblige'.

There was the little girl who was given a watch and a bottle of perfume for her birthday. She approached guests at her party by sticking her timepiece in their ears and her scented frock up to their noses. Her mummy remonstrated with her,

and the tiny tot contented herself with the announcement to all present: 'If you hear a little noise and you smell a little smell, well it's me.'

But back to nappies. You used to see toddlers sniffling, howling and walking along with a drooping, soaking, heavy nappy hanging down from one leg of plastic pants which would harden and crackle after weeks of use. Times have changed, however. It is off with the old and on with the new in a jiffy. The discarded disposables are dumped and forgotten.

Gone are the days when we used to see scores of nappies fluttering like flags on rows of washing lines. When the Lovely Maureen and I were raising our nippers, the house was always damp with the washing of nappies. They were steeping, boiling or hanging out to dry. We had a permanent rainbow in our kitchen.

And, at the risk of upsetting present-day mums, I will tell them that they don't know they are born. The nappy part of their working day has been well and truly covered. They are as pampered as their offspring, and good luck to them.

Oh, my Aching Pride

Esme is a pleasant girl. She is pretty and polite but, let's be honest about it, she will never qualify for the title Brain of Britain. Esme is happy and contented in her own sweet and innocent way. But she is — what Yorkshire folk claim — a little wet behind the ears and not exactly twelvepence to the shilling.

The lass travels daily from her home in Cleckheaton to her place of employment in Leeds and, like many girls, she grabs a quick lunch before spending the rest of her midday break window-shopping in the city centre.

It was there Esme saw the shoes. They were gaudy and cheap. But to Esme the purple, stiletto-heeled creations, with golden bows on the toecaps, were the be-all and end-all of fashionable footwear. She fell in love with them. She was demented with passion for the foppish eyesores. In her total simplicity she thought that possession of the shoes would make her the envy of all her friends. Esme was almost delirious with joyful anticipation when she headed for the shop. She clutched her purse and weekly wage, and she left the premises with a neatly wrapped box containing the light of her life.

Esme spent the weekend at home and reported for work the following Monday, when it was painfully obvious to all observers of her ungainly gait that she was having immense difficulty in walking. It was also agonisingly apparent to Esme that her feet were giving her 'gyp'. Esme's tootsies were blistered. Her 'plates' were as purple as her shoes. Her soles and heels were angry and swollen. But she lacked nothing in courage. She hobbled to work to show off her latest fashionable acquisition. And hundreds of sympathetic eyes followed her limping progress as she stumbled like a lame lobster to her perch near the assembly belt. Esme gratefully sank on to her chair. She shook her aching feet from the plastic shoes and a beaming air of relief spread over her face as she whispered: 'Thank God!'

It was the tea-break before Esme's colleagues could fathom the reason for her suffering, and the poor girl's explanation was greeted with stifled giggles. Barefooted Esme sipped her cuppa and murmured:

'I take size six in a shoe, but they didn't have a six in that colour. They didn't have a five, or even a five and a half. So I had to get fours.'

Hence the tormented toes. Esme's reasoning seemed quite logical to her, and I know that many ladies are prepared to make the ultimate sacrifice. They willingly endure intense pain in the name of haute couture, elegance, vogue and the crazy compulsion to take part in the vanity race. But Esme's illogical reasoning resulted in self-inflicted torture.

But it was Our Anne who provided the best story about footwear. Her father worked for a well-off family who often passed on 'hand-me-downs' including pretty dresses, warm coats, woollies and shoes. They were gracefully offered and gratefully received.

One day Anne came home from school for lunch with the conviction that she would spend the rest of the day at the fireside because her shoes were soaking wet. But her mum had different ideas. She rummaged in the latest cargo of 'cast-offs' to arrive from the wealthy benefactors. And she pulled out a pair of knee-length riding boots. Anne demurred at the prospect of pulling them on with the aid of little tabs sticking out of the tops of the highly-polished and calf-hugging boots. She reasoned that the only horse ever seen in her neighbourhood was the broken-down nag that reluctantly pulled Tom O'Brien's coal cart. She also knew that no girls from the hunting or horse-riding brigade actually attended St Augustine's School, off St Wilfrid's Circus, Harehills, Leeds 9. And she also feared that her sporting boots would cause no end of comment and perhaps a degree of merriment. She was not wrong. Anne — dressed like Lucinda Prior Palmer — endured a few giddy-up remarks as she marched into school in her riding boots. Her face was as crimson as the master of the foxhound's hunting pinks.

But back to Esme. I know how she felt when she first spotted those purple shoes. She had that inner compulsion to buy them. And I experienced a similar feeling as a callow youth when I spotted an imitation Crombie overcoat in a sale. I had to have it. Saturday night arrived. I dashed from the *Yorkshire Evening Post* offices where we had just put the Green Final to bed, and raced to the shop to spend my

SHOWIN' OFF THE NEW COAT AGAIN, JOHN?.!!

overtime on acquiring that super coat. It was black. It was heavy. It had spivvy built-in shoulder pads. I couldn't wait to wear it.

I arrived at the Hillcrest Cinema for the second showing of Eddie Cantor in the *Kid From Spain*. I walked the full length of the queue at least three times just to show off my imitation black and heavy Crombie with fashionable white silk scarf hanging loosely over each wide lapel. And I sweated cobs. It was a red-hot summer evening. The temperature was in the eighties. But I had to let the world know that I was the proud owner of a brand-new overcoat.

It lasted years. And certainly much longer than the excruciating shoes Esme was determined to buy, wear and endure. We both suffered from the virulent bug — pride in possession!

The Silent Heroes of Soapland

'Confession is good for the soul' was one of my late mother's enduring phrases and one recommended to all with troubled heart and mind. It is with these words of wisdom beating in my palpitating 'ticker' that I come clean and admit to the awful truth that I have been known to watch TV soaps.

Emmerdale, Eastenders and of course everyone's favourite *Coronation Street* are compulsive viewing in the Morgan household. But unlike the Lovely Maureen, who follows the adventures of various characters with sympathy, understanding and sometimes tears, my eyes search the screen for the extras — lads and lasses with walk-on roles. So many of these are friends of mine, and I know that they enjoy their fleeting moments of TV glory. They stand at the bar in the Woolpack, Queen Vic or Rovers Return, pretending to ignore the real action while they indulge in head-nodding and whispered conversations with other members of the silent acting brigade. Some are elevated to brief speaking parts, but the majority drift along content in the knowledge that they will earn a few pounds and at least friends and family will spot them on the box.

Many stand-up comedians have developed roles in soaps, and local comics Mike Kelly, Peter Wallis, Tony Heath, Joe Belcher and many others have appeared in the compelling productions.

My favourite is Jimmy O'Dea, who peers through bottle-bottom glasses as the blind-as-a-bat character in *Last Of The Summer Wine*. It is good to see such a hard-working comedian turned actor with a speaking part. There were times when Jimmy was a 'mute extra', and he always did his level best to persuade the directors to allow him to say a few words because it meant a significant increase in the wage packet.

Many still talk about the day he was cast as a doorman at a gentlemen's club. All he had to do was take a leading actor's topper and scarf as he entered the room, and walk out of camera shot. But Jimmy bowed his head and said: 'Good afternoon sir. A little better weather today, don't you think?'

The director hollered 'cut' and demanded an explanation from Jimmy, who replied: 'I have to say something to the chap out of sheer courtesy. I just can't let him in the club without passing the time of day, can I?' The man-in-charge reluctantly allowed Jimmy to insert his impromptu greeting in the script.

Another comedian not unknown in the world of soaps is Ced Beaumont, who is as well known as the bellman in his native Slaithwaite. He is also a familiar figure at dinners, clubs and concerts throughout Yorkshire, and he has appeared in many television productions, including *Heartbeat*. Ced has reached his biblical allocation of three-score-and-ten-years but he is still active on the speaking circuit, and his Yorkshire humour, tailored to suit different audiences, is always a hit with those of us who can't resist another sportsmen's function. Just before he starts his act, he pulls a flat cap from his pocket and wears it until he leaves the stage with the audience in stitches. Ced started his working life in the mills and he entered club life as a comedian to bring a little extra money into the family budget.

But Ced has one unfulfilled ambition. He would give his eye teeth to stand on the stage of the famous Leeds City Varieties and tell a few gags. And he would do it for nowt — which is a great sacrifice for a true-blooded Yorkshireman.

On the Fiddle

It was film heart-throb Stewart Grainger — fiddling in a colourful production like a demented Fritz Kreisler — who inspired my enthusiasm for the violin.

And it was always a source of deep regret that I was unable to scrape a living — or a discernible tune — from the battered instrument which I bought for £4 in a junk shop. I used to gaze at the thing of beauty with tender eyes as it lay in grimy red velvet, and I dusted and polished it with devotion. But the nerve-searing sound when I dragged the bow across badly-tuned strings was excruciating. And it struck terror in the hearts and minds of neighbours who had the misfortune to be present when my soul moved to music.

The problem was finding a violin teacher. Our housing estate was not exactly brimming with tutors. There were one or two experts who could teach fiddling of a different variety. But those who appreciated the arts were not in abundance. So I was fighting a losing battle from the word go. My fiddle lay dormant in its case for months, and eventually I reluctantly parted company with it for ten shillings. I often saw the new owner — a pupil at the nearby girls' college — proudly carrying her renovated acquisition to school where she was taught to produce beautiful melodies.

I would have given the earth had I been able to play with Max Jaffa, who enthralled so many Scarborough holiday-makers with his virtuosity. I have since courted the company of lesser violinists than Max and — if you will forgive another bout of name dropping — I will voice my admiration of the late Jimmy Wheeler and Ted Ray, who always complemented their comedy routines with a bout of fiddling.

Jimmy was part of a father and son duo called Wheeler and Wilson. They toured the Moss Empire circuit for twenty-five years. And they never changed a word of their act, which saw Jimmy play the part of a railway porter and his dad dressed as a sailor going on leave. The jolly jack tar carried a birdcage in which a bottle of Bass was attached to the swing, and Wheeler, the porter, would ask Wilson, the sailor: 'What kind of a bird is that?' His dad used to answer: 'A swallow'. And that was the standard of humour which dominated the

fifteen-minute spot which preceded Jimmy's solo act. Jimmy used to crack a few gags, play a tune called *Mistakes* and walk off the stage, still fiddling, and shouting his catch-phrase: 'Hi hi. That's your lot.'

Ted Ray was a patter comic with a gift for ad-libbing, and he played the fool, and the fiddle, with equal aplomb. But there was an occasion when he went to America to try his luck, and his act was not going at all well.

'It was my debut in vaudeville', Ted recalled. 'I cracked my first gag, which sank like the *Titanic*, and my second suffered a similar fate. Before I could continue, the biggest ripe tomato you could imagine flew from the gallery and landed smack on the starched white dicky of the orchestra conductor. Of course it was intended for me. But I turned to the irate musician who was trying to remove the red mess from his shirt and I murmured: "They don't think much to your band, do they?" The audience loved it. My joke broke the ice. I had them — and then I played my violin and lost them again. I thought they were going to lynch me.'

Ted returned home to continue his round of the music halls, which sadly started to disappear many years ago. It is to be hoped that the famous City Varieties does not meet a similar fate. Fiddling funny men like Jimmy and Ted would revolve in their resting places at the mere suggestion of such a tragedy, and no doubt Max Jaffa would join in the wake.

Watch your Language

I had been buying Nestlés chocolate for years and calling it 'Nessels', when I learnt that the proper pronunciation was 'Nestlay'. It was a bit of a shock to the old system when I heard *Look North* refer to Nestlay when it presented an item on the Swiss firm's take-over of Rowntree. I almost gave a whistle — should that be whissel or whistlay — of surprise.

Although I am not 100 per cent in favour of a phonetic language, I am the sort of chap who calls the French capital Paris and not Paree. And I was looked on with total scorn one day when I talked to a man about the Belvoir Hunt and discovered to my embarrassing horror that the proper name is 'Beaver'. There are other well-known examples like Featherstonhaugh (Fanshaw) and Cholmondely (Chumley).

In fact our lingo can be more than a little baffling at times and must be downright mysterious for visitors from abroad. How, for instance, can we expect them to differentiate between cough, bough, rough and dough?

I recall the tale of the man on a ferry. He was asleep in a lower bunk. A man in the bunk above was about to be seasick and he hollered 'Look out below'. The foreigner did and, as he made haste to the bathroom to clean himself and change his soiled nightshirt, he ranted: 'Why do you crazy English always say look out when you mean look in?'

Lord knows what he would make of a pal of mine, who named his village house the Cloister. Because it was 'cloise t' shops' and 'cloise t' pub.'

I once approached a bookie at a Yorkshire racecourse and asked if I could have £1 on Hyperbole. He looked up and down his list for the horse I had pronounced Hyperberlee. He asked me to point it out. I stuck my finger on the name and he almost exploded with indignation. 'You mean Hyperbowl', he thundered with a withering look which saw my cheeks turn scarlet and my legs resemble rubber bands.

How, I wonder, do strangers from far-off places manage when they come across an expert in cockney rhyming slang? I know one called Peter who answers to the name of 'Gas Meter'. And he always addresses me as 'Buttered', which is short for 'Buttered Scone' meaning 'John'. 'Gas' even talks in rhyming sentences and he once asked me: 'Is my boat race one hundred to thirty or is it ace, king, queen?' He was inquiring if his face was dirty or clean. And it would surely be easier to ask it as simply as that. But if he did, Yorkshire would lack another of its dwindling band of characters.

I am not entirely gone on speaking with a profound Yorkshire accent or dabbling with the dialect. I would rather say 'good nite' than 'good neet', but I can listen for hours to experts in the county's vernacular. Like the old farmer who came from the Great Yorkshire Show and announced: 'Well, if ah were goin' ageean, I wunt goa.'

Former Yorkshire cricketer Mike Cowan always amuses me with the observation: 'You must remember that TV production *It's A Knock-out*, or as the good people of Barnsley always call it, *Jeux Sans Frontieres*.'

I know what Mike means. Perhaps the folk in South Yorkshire have always said 'Nestlay' too and not 'Nessels'.

A Miracle Cure for Heartache

Do you believe in miracles? Have you ever joined your hands in pious supplication, pleaded for divine guidance, and yearned for a quick and happy solution to your problems and predicament?

I have, and so has Austin Crabtree. But Austin never dreamed of such an action until one fateful day when he was sorely troubled. He sought advice, and he eventually came to the conclusion that prayer and faith can really move mountains. But let us start at the beginning.

You must remember the story of the devout old lady Agnes who achieved a lifelong ambition when she joined an organised pilgrimage to Lourdes. Agnes enjoyed her stay which was all too short. She felt spiritually uplifted. She prayed for her family, friends and even her few foes. Agnes rewarded herself with a special gift which she stowed in the depths of her bulging suitcase. The pilgrims eventually returned home. It was time to face the customs, which was a new experience for Agnes who had never previously traversed from these shores. Agnes pushed her suitcase on a trolley and she noticed that the majority of her compatriots elected to leave by the green exit. She should have followed the trend, but she chose to pass through the red because, as she later explained with honest naivety:

'The queue was shorter. The chap in the peaked cap was not unlike Cary Grant in looks and he also appeared to be lonely. None of the passengers seemed to be stopping to talk to him.'

The official gazed on Agnes with a mixture of compassion and disbelief. But he was duty bound to demand: 'Have you anything to declare?'

He mentioned perfume, tobacco and bottles. And Agnes looked him straight in the eye and replied: 'I have nothing but a bottle of holy water.'

The non-smiling officer opened her case. He rummaged and his hand reappeared clutching her gift — a litre bottle of five-star Napoleon brandy.

'Ha ha! What's this?' he challenged.

'It's the holy water', replied Agnes.

'It's brandy', he contradicted.

'Glory be to all the saints in heaven', exclaimed Agnes, 'It's another miracle!'

It is Austin who is the star, however, and we had better get to the crux of the tale before he surrenders top billing. Austin lives in marital harmony. He has twelve tiny miracles — six boys and six girls — with barely a dozen years between the first and the latest. 'I must be stork raving mad', Austin often quips. But he worships his wife. He adores his children. He works hard to support them, and he and his devoted spouse will not be unduly worried if another infant puts in an appearance. Another mouth to feed will not promote undue hardship and it would be impossible to find a more contented chap than Austin.

But there was a time when domestic bliss and the blessings that surely accompany the plighting of the troth appeared to be a million miles away. Austin's young life was in turmoil. He had problems, and not the least was his passionate love for identical twin sisters Maria and Theresa. He was in love with both of them. Austin courted them in turn. But they were so alike he sometimes did not know whether he was out with Maria or Theresa. It was all so confusing. Austin treated them the same. He was a gentleman. His courtesy was always in evidence. He took them to the pictures and didn't even suggest that they sit in the back row. Austin always returned Maria and Theresa to their home at a decent hour. He occasionally put a protective arm round a trim waist. And when his ardour blazed he would whisper a sweet nothing before giving the girl of his dreams a gentle peck on the cheek. Austin invariably left Maria or Theresa at the garden gate, and they always turned at the kitchen door to wave a fond farewell and blow the little kiss Austin pretended to catch and place on his lips.

But he was bothered. One moment he firmly believed that he was head-over-heels in love with Maria, and the next day he would have the same all-consuming passion for Theresa. He was perplexed — off his food — and lovesick to a state of desperation. Austin decided he had to seek advice. Eventually Austin went to see his parish priest, who put a comforting arm round his shoulder and advised him to pray for help.

'The age of miracles has not yet passed, my son', the kindly cleric said. 'You will receive guidance.'

Austin disappeared into church and he returned within seconds. His face beamed utter relief.

'Golly gosh, that was quick', the good priest murmured. 'Have you decided which girl is for you?'

Austin nodded and laughed with unbridled joy. 'It's a blooming miracle, Father', he exclaimed. 'I sat in the pew, bowed my head, raised it and saw the words embroidered on the altar cloth. It was a message from Heaven. It told me to Ave Maria!'

Austin certainly did have Maria to be his lawful wedded wife, to have and to hold, for better for worse, for richer for poorer, in sickness and in health, until death do them part.

Do you believe in miracles? I do, and so does Austin.

The 'Lucky, Lucky, Lucky' Grandad

The round of social engagements threatens to rupture the spine of my bulging diary of palatable invitations. There were double-bookings, too, when it was a case of choosing between a tummy-bursting spread in a sports club or a birthday party in the Cub and Brownie hut for fifteen premature Kylie Minogues.

It was no contest. If I hadn't opted for slices of pizza, sausage rolls, chicken legs and the company of a gang of giggling eleven-year-olds, my granddaughter — the ecstatic birthday girl — would never have forgiven me. And no grandfather worth his salt would risk breaking a promise and the heart of a lovely young lady. Would he?

I remember when this trendy lassie first saw the light of day. It was at Hyde Terrace Maternity Home, and it transpired that everyone in the family — apart from yours truly — appeared to be at the bedside within minutes of the birth. They thought I was better off slumbering the sleep of the just. Folk of my ilk, and doubtful temperament, tend to panic when there is an emergency. Grandfathers have to wait in line to become an important and loving part of the newly-born.

But I soon made her acquaintance. It was noon the same day when I covered her mum's bed with fruit and flowers, peeped at the tiny bundle curled in a Moses basket, and dashed from the ward to proclaim to all and sundry: 'It's a girl. And I am her grandfather!'

Another five grandchildren have been safely delivered since that happy occasion. But you never forget the first, and it wasn't long before we battled over who would do the nursing, cooing, patting and singing — until the babe cried, of course. That is the signal for grannies and granddads to take their leave. You can't escape from the squalls, tantrums and soiled nappies of your own offspring. But you can from your children's children.

My first granddaughter progressed, and I recall with joy an incident when she was barely two years old and liked nothing better than helping to wash the pots. She would kneel on a high kitchen stool with arms plunged in a sink almost floating with soap suds. And if the lady who tells us on the television commercial that the product she advertises produces more bubbles and lasts longer than others, she never cleaned our crockery. This child would empty a bottle of foaming soap in one go, and our present pots and pans were never as clean or sparkling. The washing sessions used to last all afternoon.

It was at this stage of her introduction to domestic chores that I asked if she would like to spend a couple of days at my house to give her mum a rest. The tiny girl wriggled. She hitched up her pants, twisted a finger in her curls, hopped from one foot to another and pondered the invitation. It was a momentous decision. If she accepted, she would be spending a night away from her home for the first time. She gazed with a worried expression and then gracefully declined the offer.

'I'm sorry I can't stay. I had better get home', she murmured with an air of sincere apology. 'You see, granddad, I've got a pile of ironing to do.'

I just fell about. And I also rocked at the party at which I was detailed to act as a DJ. Fifteen girls, dressed to the nines, failed to appreciate my futile attempts to emulate Jimmy Savile and I was under orders from the young hostess not to do anything daft and show her up. Ladies of eleven tender years are fragile, often tearful for no apparent reason, affectionate to the extent of hurling their arms round each other, and profuse with their thanks for gifts of fragrant smellies, junior make-up, and tapes of Boyzone, Kylie, Spice Girls and others.

But this audience startled and surprised me. When it sat down to pop, chicken legs, quiche and chocolate buns, it was time for cabaret. But what does an ancient cabaret 'star' sing to sophisticated lasses, decked out in chic party dresses, bobby-sox and glistening shoes? Surely a pantomime sing-along number like *Why Does the Brown Cow Give White Milk When it Always Eats Green Grass* would fit the bill. It didn't. But golden-oldie music-hall favourites like *My Old Man Said Follow the Van* and *Who Were You With Last Night?* brought instant recognition and the girls joined in with great gusto. It transpired that they had learned the songs at school from one inspired teacher. She had decided to bring a little culture into musical appreciation studies, and give her

pupils an alternative to the cacophony of guitar-twanging and ear-splitting compositions which assail the ears from personal stereos and the family wireless.

The girls sang and danced. They swivelled and gyrated with *Top of the Pops* abandon. The music was loud. And tiny feet stamped with beat and rhythm. The dancers did not appreciate the 'Hi there, pop pickers' approach of this ageing swinger. But they enjoyed themselves with the joy that stems from youth in enthusiastic and boisterous flight.

I, too, actually enjoyed the birthday party — sausage rolls, pork-pies, frantic dancing and even the hysterical screams which greeted Kylie Minogue's repetitive rendition of 'Lucky, lucky, lucky'. That's how I felt, folks. Lucky and fortunate that old fuddie-duddies are accepted by the present generation of wonderful children.

Choked ... by my Underwear

The pains in an area surrounding my heart and lungs were excruciating, and worsened as the day progressed. But devotion to duty is a journalist's lot. The show had to go on.

I first experienced signs of discomfort on the drive to work, but put it down to the previous evening's over-indulgence. And, in a manner befitting a man with ink in his veins, I paid little heed to the ever-tightening constriction round my pigeon-like chest. Breathing became laboured and did not improve after my pain-killing injection of a few lunchtime pints. The brow became fevered, and I swore that if I made a miraculous recovery, I would sign the pledge.

The return drive to the bosom of the family was an agonising nightmare. I staggered from the car, removing the tie from my shirt collar, as I huffed and puffed down the garden path. I felt as though I was being strangled. The iron bands hardened round my torso and my face was as red as the proverbial beetroot.

'You look awful. But don't bring your beer and baccy troubles to me', comforted the Lovely Maureen.

'I'm in trouble', I gasped. 'I have these terrible pains. I think I am going to die.'

The Lovely Maureen's initial reaction was to dust off the insurance policies. But she decided to give me a quick examination, and told me to pull off my shirt. I did as I was bid, and she dissolved into gales of giggles.

'I'm not surprised you have chest trouble. You have the youngest child's vest on.'

I had great difficulty in pulling off the tiny cotton garment with the Cherub label and baby-size tag clearly visible. But once it was discarded, the relief was instant and welcome.

I remembered that the alarm had not rung that morning and I was in danger of being late for work. I had dressed in the dark and grabbed clean pants and vest from the clothes horse without looking ... hence the youngster's vest, the trouble with my chest, possible stroke and heart attack, and the threat of a premature exit from this wonderful world.

It was probably a throwback to my childhood, when it was a case of 'first up — best dressed'. We were summoned at

what we thought was the crack of dawn. You would stretch a tentative toe from under the blankets and test the temperature of the linoleum, retreat to the warmth of the covers, and wait for the desperate call which warned you were already ten minutes late for school. You dragged yourself wearily down the 'wooden hills', peeling off pyjamas (there's swank for you), only to discover that one or other of your brothers had pinched your shirt or jersey.

Eiderdowns were a bit of a luxury in some households. And you must have heard the story of the kiddies who shared a bed with an overcoat slung on the top for extra insulation and bodily comfort. Visitors arrived, and the mother of the house was red-faced when Johnny shouted: 'The overcoat has dropped off the bed.' Mother ran up the 'dancers', replaced the fallen garment and snapped at her offspring: 'It is not an overcoat. It is an eiderdown. Remember that.' She returned to make a cup of tea for her callers when Johnny's voice rang out again.

'Our Herbert has pulled the sleeve off the eiderdown, mum', he bawled.

We always had a surfeit of underclothes. My mother was not too worried about what went on top. But — like the majority of doting mums — she was anxious about the clobber nearest the skin.

'I hope you have clean pants and vest on in case you get knocked down', was her inevitable parting shot.

I don't think our maternal parent was as concerned about our physical welfare as the possibility of our undies being exposed to nosy neighbours and others.

Mothers used to tell us that cleanliness was next to godliness, and my goodness me how they worried about the state of their laundry. We had a set-pot which was on twice and sometimes three times a week to cope with the never-ending pile of dirty clothes. Do you remember the rubbing with carbolic soap and a dip of dolly blue to turn everything whiter than white? That sometimes applied to the colours too. I once spent months in pink underclothes because our Kitty's blouse, of that rosy hue, became mixed with the heavier wash and lost its colour to our undies. When it came to stripping for gymnasium activities, I received some very strange glances from my athletic colleagues.

Muscles ached from turning the old-fashioned mangle with its cast-iron surrounds and strong wooden rollers which squeezed excess water from the laundered clothes before they were pegged into a colourful splash of fluttering 'weshing' on groaning lines. A prop was placed under the suspended clothes to force them to the rooftops where they flew like the flags at a naval review of the fleet. When high-topped vans or lorries came down the road it was God help the driver who didn't honk his horn to signal his arrival. Ladies would scamper from the house to remove the dangling laundry and allow the vehicle to proceed.

I hated washdays. The house always smelled of soap, bleach and starch. And it was a heaven-sent facility when the launderettes opened.

I don't wear vests these days, although my breath still comes in short pants.

Panacea For a Few Pence

The chap wore an agonised expression of self-pity. He rubbed his tender tummy as he entered the chemist's shop. He walked to the counter, banged the bell with the flat of his hand, and pleaded:

'I've got a dicky stomach and these griping pains are killing me. Can you make me something up?'

'Certainly', the chemist replied. And he opened one of a hundred tiny drawers to search for a suitable potion. He extracted the remedy and murmured: 'By the way, Frank Sinatra called in here yesterday.'

'He didn't, did he?' the stricken customer gasped.

'No, he didn't. I made it up', the chemist smiled.

But there is a certain cure for all complaints. A good sweat was always recommended for every illness when I was a child, and I still believe in the logical remedy that perspiration — buckets of it — is a proper prescription for poorly people.

Before the advent of National Health, it was not everyone who could meet the cost of a doctor visiting or even pay for surgery treatment and prescriptions. I remember 'doctor's bills' and how they were collected by weekly subscriptions until the account was settled. Treatment was not always within the financial reach of some people, and they sought advice from the local chemist and bought his valued medicine for a few pence.

Bells Old Pharmacy, Kirkgate, Leeds, used to be packed with ladies seeking potions, pills and powders for the family ailments. The proprietor Mr Bentley had several 'magical' cures and concoctions for the relief of one pain or another. And he sold a special liquid for soothing the fretting and teething babies.

Gripe water and Nurse Harvey's Mixture were for the offspring of the well-heeled. Mums with lesser income opted for a bottle of Mr Bentley's 'Diddle Um'. He brewed gallons of the nectar. And it certainly diddled the kiddies. One minute a child would be as scarlet as a boiled beetroot. His nose ran, eyes streamed, and gums were inflamed and angry as his little fist rubbed the affected parts. The babe would

make the night hideous with squalls designed to awaken the neighbourhood. But one swig of 'Diddle Um' usually did the trick. No-one will ever know what Mr Bentley put in his elixir. But it certainly contained knockout drops. A pacified peace descended on the scene. The baby was concussed. The infant slept like a man with a pain-killing injection of ten pints of Tetleys. And 'Diddle Um' rarely failed. Baby would awake to burp from either or both ends, and adopt the glazed look of a boxer recovering from a right hook. 'What hit me?' babies appeared to ask, and they were usually quiet — poleaxed is a better word — for the rest of the day, only to burst into screaming life at some impossible hour to holler for dad, mum and another dose of 'Diddle Um'.

I often ran errands for neighbours to Bells Old Pharmacy, asking for 'A bottle of "Diddle-Um", please. Mrs So-and-so wants to get the baby's windies up.'

But this was not the only home-made formula dispensed by Mr Bentley and his staff. Customers confided: 'Mr Bentley is better than any doctor. He knows more than any of them.' And they sought his advice on all things medical, and had implicit faith in the tonics and tablets he mixed in his dispensary.

Of course we had other remedies, too, some of them home made. We had sweaty socks to wrap round sore throats. We had bread poultices plastered on our chests, and you stuck your feet in mustard baths to relieve chills, colds and, some claimed, pneumonia. We had Carnation corn-plasters for the girls who ruined their toes by wearing too-tight shoes. We had iron calipers for children born with deformed legs, and basket chairs for invalids. They had two wheels at the back, one in the front, and the passenger steered it with a type of joy-stick as you pushed like the clappers from behind.

But there is one pill which will always stick in my mind if not in my throat. The name Vocalzones may not be as well known as Fishermen's Friends, Zubes, Victory V Lozenges or Little Imps — all designed to inflame the tongue and give you breath hot enough to burn toast. Vocalzones carried the label 'As prescribed for the world-famous Italian tenor Enrico Caruso'. That testimony alone was sufficient to send budding opera stars — like myself — haring to the chemists for a tin or two. I used to suck a Vocalzone and launch into *O Sole Mio* and *Your Tiny Hand is Frozen* with renewed confidence in my lungs and tonsils. Saturday nights invariably meant a trip to the pictures, and necessitated a Vocalzone and a lick of Brylcreem. I can assure you that I used my acquired Latin looks and matching voice to all-conquering purpose. Many a lovely lass fell to my *Come Back to Sorrento* thanks to Vocalzones.

I break into a sweat at the thought of those far-off days ... and melodious nights.

The Bug Hutch

The Western Cinema was my Saturday 'bug hutch', where we howled at the antics of Old Mother Riley, George Formby, the Keystone Kops and grumpy Edgar Kennedy.

We cheered cavalrymen who always arrived in the nick of time to rescue besieged pioneers squatting behind a circle of wagons. Every single pot-shot our hero aimed accounted for half-a-dozen fiendish Indians; but there were always scores more to take their place. We crossed our legs with terror when Bela Lugosi and Boris Karloff gripped our vivid imaginations with *The Clutching Hand, Dracula* and *The Mummy Walks Again*. We oohed and aahed when Rin Tin Tin and Lassie performed canine acts of uncanny kindness. We soft-shoe-shuffled when hundreds of dancers tapped out a rhythmic beat in *George White Scandals*. And we lived in a dream world for a couple of brief hours when Deanna Durbin, or Nelson Eddy or Jeanette MacDonald, warbled love songs.

I can still see Mother Riley rolling up her sleeves at the sight of daughter Kitty's boyfriend. She shouted: 'I'll murder him. I'll murder him.' I can hear Kitty McShane asking: 'How long will supper be, mother?' Old Mother Riley replied: 'Six inches — it's a sausage.'

But my lasting memory of the Western is not of the pictures but of a regular patron called Leonard.

The Western opened as the Harehills Cinema before the First World War. It changed its name to the Western Talkie before it became the Vogue. We formed long queues for the matinee, but Leonard never took his turn. If he wanted to walk to the front, no-one argued. We were — as one pal put it — 'freetened to death of him'.

Many children had deformed legs with rickets, but poor Leonard had crippled limbs and a terribly bent back. He hobbled with the help of sticks. He usually had a dew-drop on the end of his nose, and he sucked on the tab-end of a cigarette which he offered round and growled 'Have a swallow'.

Leonard put the fear of God in me. I ran a mile when he came into view, and it was because of his regular patronage of the Western I opted for the Hillcrest instead. I was with my

sister Kitty. We queued down a long dingy passage for entrance to the cheapest rows. We dashed into the darkness, sat down, and an untidy bundle moved in the next seat to 'our lass'. It was Leonard ... and we flew!

He was harmless, and so was Alan — a Peter Pan-type of lad who never grew old — and even when he reached manhood he still wore short trousers and a schoolboy cap.

Alan was a regular at the Regal, Crossgates, where he occupied a front seat and shouted encouragement to the cowboys and booed the opposition. He usually had the front row to himself because one blood-curdling shout from Alan was sufficient for unsuspecting young patrons of the matinees to flee to other parts of the cinema or race for the exit.

Unlike the Western, the Regal had upholstered seats — not wooden forms on which you had to 'budge up' as more customers arrived. The Regal also had a chap who made occasional tours of the interior squirting a perfumed spray which at least camouflaged other aromas pertinent to picture houses when the 'penny crush' was in business.

I haven't been to 'the flicks' for years. The last picture I saw was so old, Gabby Hayes got the girl.

Memoirs of a Brylcreem Boy

I wasn't old enough to be one of the Battle of Britain's 'Glorious Few'. But I was one of the many who basked in the reflected glory of the Royal Air Force achievement when I answered the call from the late King George VI to serve my country as a national serviceman.

But I was a reluctant airman second class. I had the role of Brylcreem boy thrust on me. I was tied to the apron strings. And it was a wrench to snap the family links and head for Padgate, near Warrington, for kitting out.

We marched! There's a laugh. Half the new contingent of recruits lacked co-ordination. The ungainly gait gave them the appearance of out-of-control marionettes, and the jerky action was not improved with the donning of ill-fitting uniforms.

I can still smell the blanco we smeared on our packs and straps. I can almost taste the black boot-polish we basted with hot knife-blades into the 'bulling' of boots. I can remember the polishing of bed-spaces and the scrubbing of billet tables. I recall the whitened surrounds of the antiquated fireplaces in the centre of our communal bedrooms, the fashioning of folded blankets and sheets into squares, and the fuming rage of a non-commissioned officer if he spotted a hair out of place or a wrinkle in our bedpack.

The rule was that if it moved, you saluted. If it did not move, you picked it up and took it with you. If it was too big to pick up, you painted it — white!

Life was not without humour. I remember sitting in the Padgate reception area where an officer bade us welcome to the Royal Air Force and asked forty quaking recruits — miserable and wet behind the ears — to fill in a questionnaire. He pinned an enlarged copy of the form on to a blackboard and gave us his example of how to write down the answers.

'For instance, you put in your number, 12345 etcetera', he said, 'then your name Joe Soap, and your rank, AC2 etcetera'.

Believe it or not, but at least half of the lads penned the answers: '12345 etcetera, Joe Soap, and AC2 etcetera'. The officer collected the forms. He glanced at the answers and threw an apoplectic fit.

Shortly after that outburst, I was posted to West Kirby to meet the man who was destined to dominate my waking hours and give me nightmares for the next six weeks. He was the chap with the job of knocking all things civilian out of his charges and changing us from yokels into ultra-smart, disciplined, well-drilled airmen. He fought a losing battle in my case.

His name was Flight Sergeant Loban. He was hewn in Glasgow. He had tartan-coloured eyes and a voice with the harshness of shrapnel. He hated national servicemen. And he detested me with a malice bordering on mouth-foaming frenzy. He opened his mouth like the nearby Mersey Tunnel to scream at me. He handed out jankers (punishments) with scant regard for RAF standing orders. He was judge and jury. He once detailed me to scrub the latrines — the wash-house and toilets — with a toothbrush. He was quite mad.

I first fell foul of him when I was on guard duty. I stood at the entrance to the camp with my rifle and bayonet at the ready. But instead of halting a car — driven by a peak-capped chap — I presented arms in salute and allowed him to enter unchallenged. He turned out to be a taxi driver. And Flight Sergeant Loban had witnessed the lot. From that moment my life became round-the-clock torment and misery. And he threatened: 'One day I will kill you for showing up the RAF.'

You can imagine the joyous relief when my departure from West Kirby was confirmed, but my leaving had one final moment of horror. I leaned out of a speeding vehicle to wave goodbye to my favourite flight sergeant, but he must have misconstrued my cheerio gesture as a 'Harvey Smith'. He gave chase and he nearly caught us when the bus slowed to a halt at the guard room checkpoint. We eventually arrived at Lime Street Station, Liverpool, to catch trains to our respective homes, and my blood ran cold when I spotted Loban prowling the platforms. Pals and even strangers — aware of the situation — surrounded my crouching figure and smuggled me to the safety of the Leeds-bound locomotive. I sweated cobs until the engine steamed out of Flight Sergeant Loban's evil-eyed sight.

When my short leave was over, I was in two minds about going back. I felt like taking a leaf from the book of a neighbour's lad who never rejoined his regiment without the

persuasion of a couple of military policemen. When he returned to the bosom of his family for the statutory seventy-two hours, you could bet your life that the 'vacation' would last weeks. His mother was always glad to see him. But she was not at all pleased when his pass expired because he was a greedy drain on the limited family ration of wartime groceries. He used to eat her out of house and home.

There was one occasion when the army police arrived to ask if she had seen her lad, who always hid from view by standing in the window with voluminous draw-curtains wrapped round him. The soldier's mum shouted so her son could hear:

'No, I haven't seen him. He's not here.'

But what her beloved offspring did not know was that she was indicating with flickering eyes, broad winks and pointing fingers to his whereabouts. The bobbies charged into the front room, undraped the runaway, and he was taken to the glasshouse before his return to duty. After six or seven similar arrests, he twigged what his mum was doing, and as he — and the escorting redcaps — passed her he hissed 'Judas'.

He was not one of the few. He didn't want to be a hero. I shared his reticence. But I will always voice unstinting praise and gratitude to those who paid the ultimate price to make Britain a safe haven for you, me and our offspring.

When Opportunity Knocked

Clubland enjoyed a boom time in the era when young journalists wore imitation Harris tweed jackets with patches on the elbows, and a fountain pen and matching pencil clipped in the top pocket.

A television programme, *Opportunity Knocks*, fronted by Hughie Green, gave young artistes the chance to display their many talents. Hughie toured the nation auditioning singers, dancers, comics and speciality acts, and many soared to stardom to become household names here and abroad.

One of Hughie's greatest 'finds' was Engelbert Humperdinck. It was obvious when he sang at the Fforde Greene Pub, Harehills, Leeds, and at the Ace of Clubs, Woodhouse Street, Leeds, that he was destined to perform at more glittering venues. I often wonder if Engelbert thinks back to the days of theatrical digs in Spencer Place, Leeds, or the time he was taken to a Leeds hospital with suspected tuberculosis.

Engelbert also drew a few screams of adulation from female fans in a Bradford club where he followed an unknown comic who had a line in patter straight from the land of blarney. The comedian was Frank Carson, who came off stage, drank a glass of stout, and returned to ask if any member of the audience could give him a lift to his next engagement in Leeds. He was 'doubling' at the Ace of Clubs and a gentleman of the press volunteered to drive him. It was me. Frank slumbered throughout the journey, and within minutes of his arrival he was cracking gags — as only he can tell 'em.

We had a surfeit of comics, including one Pat Mooney — another Irish chap — who never forgot the introduction he was given at a club in the North East. Pat said:

'The concert secretary asked the audience: "Who is the best comic round here and how much do we pay him?" The members shouted: "Bobby Knoxall and he gets twenty-five quid". The concert secretary hollered: "Well, this Irish feller must be brilliant because he is on thirty. Welcome, if you will, Pat Mooney". The audience gasped and I walked on stage to silence. I did my act and tried my hardest, but died a death. There was silence which turned to abuse, and eventually I had a police escort to safety.'

But the world of working men's clubland was a magical attraction for members, and my old friend Sam Wood recalls the time when concerts were a weekend highlight:

'In the days before television exerted such a hold on our lives, the local club provided first-class entertainment. Microphones were not essential because singers, duettists and comedians knew how to project their voices. They could be heard even at the back of the concert rooms.

Comics were not allowed to tell smutty jokes. If they did, they were paid off and barred from future bookings.

I remember popular turns like Billy Butler, who always came on stage holding a stuffed chicken, Hal Martin and Billy Williams, Dolly Bulmer, Maxam Harcourt, and Bob Bradley who mimed to *Figaro*.

I also remember Bob as the man who sang to the record *Mule Train* and repeatedly hit himself on the head with a tin tray. Bob was brilliant, and he made his farewell appearance on a Michael Barrymore show a few years ago. He was just one of many stars of clubland.

The Worm Turns

Bob is an easy-going chap. A more fitting description would be amiable, shrinking, or simply meek and mild.

He doesn't want the earth. All he requires is time to potter in his trim garden, walk the dog and make an occasional sortie to the local for his half of lager. Bob nods agreement when you volunteer 'Nice day'. He rarely contributes to the conversation. Bob is a listener. He sips his drink and occasionally tut-tuts when the talk becomes a little animated.

But Bob blew his top the other night. Without any preamble. Without the semblance of an introductory note. Without any warning, but with mouth twitching, eyes rotating, and neck and forehead veins protruding, he barked:

'I told the wife tonight. I let her have it straight!'

It was so out of character. Regulars nearly dropped their glasses halfway through a gulping swallow of the light brown nectar. One choked on his pint. He stuttered and spluttered. He had to be given a couple of hearty clouts in the middle of his back to aid recovery from the shock of Bob's totally unexpected burst of verbal violence.

We waited with silent expectancy for Bob to continue. We exchanged worried glances. We read each other's thoughts. We wondered in anxious unity. What in God's name had Bob done? Had he flipped or had he been at the sherry bottle? Had he sniffed the boots and apron worn by our ever-pickled barman, Charlie? We waited with the proverbial baited breath for Bob to elaborate on his newly-spawned explosive image.

Bob took a pull at his lager. It wasn't the usual sip. The soles of his shoes beat a rapid tattoo on the parquet floor of our rather posh tap-room. He panted with emotion. His knuckles whitened as fingers gripped the empty glass. The worm had obviously turned.

'I told Jean straight tonight', he repeated. 'I shouted that I wasn't standing for it. And I won't. Take it from me ... I won't!'

You could have heard a flea hiccup. Domino players stopped shuffling. Members of the dart-throwing ranks stayed the hands that sling those arrows of outrageous

fortune. And our landlord thrust his brandy glass under the optic with the careless abandon of a man prepared — for once only — to pay for his own drink.

Bob gazed at the ring of froth at the base of his glass. His eyes roamed round the stunned audience. He puffed out his pigeon chest and he continued:

'I told Jean tonight that if she didn't buy me a brand-new pan scrubber, she would have to do the washing up herself tomorrow!'

The silence was deafening. We looked with mingled mirth, pity and no small measure of admiration at Bob — the man of the moment. And I immediately proposed him for life membership of the henpecked club.

I have a work colleague who goes into his garage twice a night after telling his trusting loved one — a lady who is anti-smoking — that he is checking the engine and making a few minor but essential adjustments. He doesn't even raise the bonnet. Instead he smokes a couple of cigarettes. After his surreptitious pull on the weed, he disperses the vapours and returns to his lounge, the company of an appreciative spouse, and her statutory allowance of one small whisky. She doesn't know he has two large scotches before her arrival from work each evening. And his wife often compliments him on his 'engineering skill' when the car purrs into action.

She occasionally looks at the whisky bottle, notes the level of the contents, and knows — because he told her years ago — that good whisky becomes paler once the cork has been removed. He has never enlightened her to the fact that he replaces the doubles with water. But he concedes to confidants — like me — that the beverage lacks its usual kick as he gets to the bottom of the bottle.

Such subterfuge. Is it all worth it? If you are like Bob, or my colleague, you will probably answer in the affirmative and subscribe to the maxim: 'Anything for a quiet life'.

But I also have one or two potential rakes and roués in my wide circle of ever-intriguing acquaintances.

There is Geoffrey boy, who twice in the last ten years has used the same ruse to excuse his later than late return to the bosom of his family. It was 1.30am when he drove up his drive. He parked the car, plunged into a clump of evergreens, deliberately dirtied his hands, shirt cuffs and the knees of his trousers, and entered home with the cry:

'That ruddy car. I've had a puncture. Had to change the wheel myself. Couldn't get through to the AA. The fellow that tightened the nuts must have been a gorilla. I'm fair whacked. I'm sorry I'm late ... is that the time? I haven't eaten a thing.'

The dishevelled appearance and torrent of plausible reasons for his sins have — on both occasions — been met with sympathy, understanding and absolution.

But none will ever match, or beat, the excuse employed by another mate who had spent the night in doubtful company. He woke at 6.30am after his dalliance. He picked up the telephone, dialled his worried wife and screamed with relieved exultation: 'Don't pay the ransom, Mary. I've escaped!'

I do hope that Bob has got his new pan-scrubber. The Lovely Maureen never has such problems with me. I'm a model husband. 'Yes, you model for Toby jugs', she hissed.

Pulling the Other One

The discovery of nylon revolutionised ladies' legwear and other unmentionables. Before this miracle material, ladies wore silk or lisle stockings. And, if you went home from school and noticed that your mother had only one stocking on, you would guess with a decree of certainty: 'It will be jam roly-poly for pudding tonight.'

I never liked tights. If you do a bank raid, you have to take a pal with you! I much prefer stockings, which have so many uses apart from the conventional purpose of covering and beautifying ladies' limbs.

Just after the war, flour was lumpy, rough in texture and grey in colour. Housewives who did their own baking transformed the wholemeal-type flour — so fashionable now — into a white, smooth, almost powdery consistency, for baking good Yorkshire bread. They used nylons as a sieve. You saved a used or laddered nylon, cut off the foot, tied a knot, filled it with flour and patted the same over a bowl. Out came the virginal flour ready for the mixing.

A pal of mine also wears nylons. I asked him how long this had been going on.

'Ever since the wife found a pair in the back of my car', he replied.

Town of Good Manners

Shopping in Harrogate with the Lovely Maureen is an occasional 'treat', and it is almost a pleasure to spend money in this equally delightful town. Assistants are genteel, helpful and courteous. But one shop-walker in a men's department was perhaps a trifle too gushing when he asked: 'What is sir's pleasure?'

'Sir' was tempted to reply — as a Yorkshire farmer did in Harrods — 'Greyhound racing, pigeons and rugby league. Now get me a cap.'

But sirs do not say that sort of thing in Harrogate, one of Yorkshire's principal contributors to tourism, and one of the country's finest conference centres.

I had to smile when I spotted a trio extracting ready cash from one of the 'banks in the wall'. They were dressed as Cromwellians, escapees from the encampment surrounding Ripley Castle for a friendly weekend siege of that historic edifice. One of the trio opened the pouch attached to his leather belt. He pulled out a plastic card, inserted it in the 'bank', and drew enough cash for himself and friends. The man turned to a smiling audience, held aloft his cash card and hollered: 'Do not scoff, good citizens. Even Oliver Cromwell had one of these.'

Having a Beano

Hands up all the doting dads who enjoy nothing more than a sneak peep at kiddies' comics. There were times when I could hardly wait for my offspring to climb the wooden hills and leave behind the captivating adventures of Lord Snooty, Spanky McFarland and Korky the Cat.

But I kicked my addiction to the *Dandy* and *Beano* a few years ago — until I picked up a modern publication. I nearly blew a fuse. There was no front-page Dennis the Menace — just a slimy creature with warts, horns and tentacles attempting to embrace an equally gruesome beast. And this grisly pair were the goodies!

My thoughts immediately turned to schoolboy days, when Saturday mornings permitted an extra hour in bed with such compelling reading as *Film Fun*, *Chips* and *Funny Wonder*. Swapping comics was the norm. Single copies of the *Wizard*, *Adventure*, *Rover* and, much later, the *Eagle*, with intrepid Dan Dare, would be read by scores of lads.

I graduated from *Funny Wonder*, with those lazy tramps Tired Tim and Weary Willie, to *Film Fun*, which starred

the loveable duo Laurel and Hardy. There was always a burglar in this strip cartoon. He was drawn with a flat cap, hooped jersey and black eye-mask. He invariably carried a bag over his shoulder with the letters SWAG clearly visible. There was usually a candelabra and other silverware sticking from the neck of the sack of booty, and he inevitably got his just deserts. Laurel and Hardy were hard up. They used to stand outside the Hotel de Posh and stare like a couple of Bisto kids at diners, in dinner jackets, tucking into mounds of mashed potatoes from which sausages stuck out like chapel hat-pegs. Corks flew from bottles marked POP and drenched swells held ribboned boxes with CHOCS printed on the lids. You could fairly see our heroes drooling at the mouth as they gazed at the sumptuous scene.

Desperate Dan was my favourite cartoon character. His cow pies even had the horns of the bull rising from the thick crust, and his bristled jaw jutted as he perched with knife and fork at the ready.

The *Wizard,* of course, had Wilson the all-round sportsman, who could bowl out Australia, crack the winning run, throw a javelin out of sight, outspeed the world's fastest runners and swim the Atlantic before returning to his lonely life in the wilderness. I think he would have beaten Alf Tupper — the tough of the track — if that challenge had ever been issued. Alf was the athlete who trained on a diet of fish and chips. And he was just as gifted at his chosen sport as Limpalong Leslie, the Cannonball Kid and Roy of the Rovers were at football.

Good always triumphed over evil in the stories. The square-shooting guys like Roy Rogers, Gene Autry, Tom Mix, Buck Jones, Johnny Mack Brown and — my favourite — Ken Maynard always came up trumps. They were winners but modest about their achievements. The Lone Ranger even wore a mask to hide his identity.

I think I'll stop up late tonight and read my old copy of *Chick's Own.*

An Elusive Crock of Gold

Although my pal Charlie dabbles on the football pools, he rarely checks his copy coupon. He trusts those who receive his weekly perm — always on the same numbers. He is convinced they will send a representative to inform him of how much he has won when that inevitable stroke of good fortune occurs.

Charlie is ultra-confident that the elusive crock of gold will eventually come his way, and you can imagine the excitement when an urgent knock at his front door was accompanied by the holler 'I'm from Littlewoods'. Charlie bounded from the comfort of his armchair. He mentally counted his winnings as he hurtled from the lounge and he opened the door to greet the man with portfolio. The rep repeated: 'I'm from Littlewoods and ...' That is as far as he got.

Charlie let out a whoop of ecstatic delight and shouted to his better half Sally: 'We're rich. We've won the pools. I knew it was only a question of time.'

The visitor coughed and brought Charlie down to earth with the added information: 'I'm from Littlewoods catalogues. We haven't received your wife's last payment for the club she is running.'

Poor Charlie! His life was in ruins. He walked slowly back to his chair — a sadder, wiser and broken man. He is skint. But he is still optimistic about his numbers coming up. He is sure that one day he will hit the jackpot and he — and Sally — will live in idle luxury for the rest of their days.

It is a dream we all have. When I can't sleep, I pretend that I have won a million pounds from my football flutter or even that amount from the National Lottery. And I immediately start giving it away. There is quite a handsome sum for the Lovely Maureen. I build and pay for houses for my sons and daughter. I guarantee the financial future of the grandchildren, and I make handsome donations to differing charities — all deserving causes and all worthy of my largesse. I drift back into slumberland with a contented mind and a happy heart, and wake again to find nowt in my pocket but the linings of the trousers I bought from St Gemma's charity shop.

I tend to think that we are all obsessed with money, and those with an endless supply of the stuff will assure us that it definitely is the root of all evil. If it is, why don't they send oodles of it our way and let us put the claim to the acid test?

We seem to be chasing our financial tail from the day we are born. I am sure we are in debt from birth and, if some banks had their way, we certainly would be. My nine-year-old granddaughter received a communication from one of the Big Five. It offered her an instant loan up to £7,000, without a charge on her property. And it very kindly gave her ample time to pay back her windfall. At least the bank manager had a sense of humour. When he was informed of my little girl's age, he quipped:

'I am afraid it is another example of our new computer continuing its reign of error.'

I remember contacting a bank chief for a mortgage which, as every borrower knows, is another term for a 'home groan'. I wrote:

'If you can see your way clear to giving me an overdraft, I shall be forever in your debt.'

My pathetic attempt at jollity failed to impress the holder of the purse, and I was forced to take my begging bowl elsewhere.

But money isn't everything. I once had the job of interviewing the late Charles Engelhard, on whom Ian Fleming based his fictional character Goldfinger. Mr Engelhard had everything that money can buy, with one exception. He was able to indulge his passion for works of art, beautiful ladies, thoroughbred racehorses, sleek yachts and luxurious mansions. But he could not purchase good health. When I met him, his bulky frame oozed sweat and fat. He had difficulty walking. He had a retinue of doctors and nurses. He had just won the Derby and he celebrated with half a tumbler of sugar-free cola. Mr Engelhard was a sad sight, with the perspiration streaming in rivulets from under his top hat leaving damp patches on a shirt collar which threatened to burst from round his swollen neck. Immediately after sipping his cola, he was whisked back to a London hotel room to rest. And his hangers-on drank to the owner's racing triumph and painted the town all colours of the rainbow.

But back to the pools. I've done them for 'yonks' without as much as a sniff of a fortune, although I have rubbed shoulders with many who succeeded. My late colleague Arthur Day and I were present when Vivian Nicholson riffled her hands through a rail of silken frocks and murmured the immortal words: 'I'm going to spend, spend, spend!'

I also heard of the chap with a weak heart who landed a mammoth dividend. But his family thought it unwise to tell him because the shock might be too much for his dicky ticker. They summoned the family doctor to break the news. The man of medicine was an expert and trained in such matters. He had the perfect bedside manner. The doctor murmured gently to his patient: 'If you won the pools, what would you do?' The invalid replied: 'I'd give half to you.' The doctor was so taken aback he dropped dead.

I don't believe it for one moment. And neither do I believe that immense riches will one day be mine. I can't even contemplate the possibility of the man from Littlewoods rapping on my door. But I count my blessings and they are more precious than monetary wealth. I do hope you are in the same fortunate position.

The Virtues of Home

Filey beach was deserted. The weather was not too good. But a brisk walk on the prom was an ideal way to get rid of the city cobwebs. It was even pleasant to sniff the mixed odours of fish and diesel at Coble Landing.

Hotels and boarding houses displayed, with more hope than confidence, the sign 'Vacancies'. Other 'digs' signalled finality with the notice 'For Sale' spelling the end of a dream and ownership of a thriving little place by the seaside.

'We have to live in the winter when you've gone', was often the plaintive cry from boarding-house proprietors.

But the summers appear to be shorter and wetter, and the winters decidedly longer. British resorts cannot guarantee one essential holiday ingredient — sunshine. And the ever-increasing evacuation of these shores for sunnier climes will continue to increase in volume and momentum.

But there is much to be said for holidays in Britain. Where can you match the rolling splendour of the Dales and Lakes? How can you desert the picturesque glories of Yorkshire and even parts of Lancashire? You will never be eaten alive by mosquitos and the like. You will not have to worry about tap

AT LEAST THERE'S
NO MOSQUITOS !!

water. You will not be concerned about the perils of stomach bugs. The bobby on the beat will not be a gun-toting keeper of the peace, and begging will be restricted to mail received by pools and Lottery winners. In fact, I would rather spend winter in Filey than summer in many of the foreign, plastic-packed, artificial spots where folk pay for a blistered back as a painful prelude to a bout of skin-peeling.

Yorkshire's seaside towns will be described by many as the 'last resort'. But they remain number one in our childhood memories. Maybe we should start backing Britain again. There's much to be said in favour of the old countryside and coastal attractions. And Yorkshire has more than its fair share of these God-given delights. Perhaps we tend to ignore the beauty on our doorstep. It is high time we realised that our grass is greener and our sands the equal of any when it comes to making castles in kind or in the air.

It was an American visitor to Kilburn, near Thirsk, who drew my attention to the magnificent scenery many of us take for granted. He toured the 'Mousey' Thompson furniture factory and settled on a bench outside the Forresters Arms, drank a pint of beer, and reflected on the village overlooked by the famous White Horse. He smacked his lips and murmured: 'Paradise, paradise.'

The tourist asked the Forresters Arms landlord John Mayne if there was any history attached to the mighty oak tree spreading its rich abundance of foliage in front of the hostelry. Always ready to oblige with a piece of country lore — true or otherwise — John said: 'That tree is famous because the highwayman Dick Turpin hid among the branches and escaped from the policemen who chased him as he rode his mare Black Bess from London to York.' The American was most impressed. His wife expressed a similar reaction and murmured 'Gee'. Twelve months later, a coach arrived at Kilburn and disgorged three dozen holidaymakers from all parts of the United States. 'We are here to see Tip Durkin's tree', explained the excited leader of the party.

John Mayne has gone to his heavenly reward. But the pub, tree and legend lives on as one of our county's most picturesque and welcoming attractions.

Who needs to go abroad? Not me.